first interview

Also Published by Navigator Consulting

Sydney Recruitment Industry Performance Report

Melbourne Recruitment Industry Performance Report

first interview
by Tony Hall

First Interview is the work of leading recruitment industry management consultant Tony Hall.

Tony holds an Economics degree and an MBA from New Orleans in the US. As a former Ernst & Young management consultant he has held several senior sales and marketing positions in Australia and overseas.

He is managing director of Navigator Consulting and an experienced strategy consultant, conference speaker, board member and trainer, having worked with a diverse range of recruitment firms.

He facilitates Captain's Table (a recruitment industry owner's management group), publishes the annual Recruitment Industry Performance Report and is prominent among the most knowledgeable recruitment industry management consultants in Australia.

Published by

Navigator Consulting Group Pty Ltd
Specialist Recruitment Industry Researchers and Management
Consultants

Suite 17, 1 Cranbrook Ave, Cremorne NSW 2090, Australia
Tel +61 2 9904 1474   Fax +61 2 9904 4642
Email thall@navigatorconsult.com

© 2000 Navigator Consulting Group Pty Ltd ABN 68 081 368 685

ISBN 0-646-39996-9

Introduction and Acknowledgments

First Interview is a unique collection of the most inspiring and humbling stories from Australia's leading recruiters. The book recognises a group of professionals who have achieved extraordinary success and continue to provide inspiration to thousands of staff members, clients and candidates.

Of course not all of Australia's best are included in this book. Those included were selected from various surveys and recommendations. No doubt there are many others who deserve recognition and have ideas to share with the industry. To this end we have included a nomination form at the back for you to propose recruiters for our next book - Second Interview - which will feature some of our rising stars and quiet achievers.

Special thanks go to editor Lea Eldridge of Thumbnail who did a fantastic job.

We are very grateful to Andrew Hall and his highly professional production team at Advertising Energy including Chelli Kover, Juanita Jones, Sally Watts and the excellent designer Kerr Vernon.

Thanks also to Julie Mills and Kirsten Warren of the RCSA for their support and encouragement, compilers Jaide Olive, Louise Houston and proof-reader Michael Hall of Cap Gemini Ernst & Young.

Our corporate sponsors have been key to ensuring the quality of First Interview. We are very grateful to leading recruitment industry service providers Advertising Energy, Dialog Information Technology, Scott Recruitment Services and Macquarie Bank who all instantly saw the value of compiling this important collection of advice from recruitment leaders.

Recruiters and managers – it's all here. Everything you need to know on your path to the top of one of Australia's most dynamic and exciting professions.

Index

Andrew Banks

Well-known recruitment identity Andrew Banks started his career in the industry in 1980 with Slade Consulting in Sydney. He moved to Brisbane in 1982 and assumed the role of Northern Regional Manager. Leaving the company in late 1984 he established Morgan & Banks with Geoff Morgan and Ian Burns in January 1985.

They sold the company to Select Appointments in 1988 in order to manage expansion in the northern hemisphere but bought back the company in 1990, rescuing it from the brink of receivership.

he Morgan & Banks team floated in 1994 with market capitalisation of $30 million and then merged with TMP Worldwide in February 1999 for a valuation of $330 million. By that time the Morgan & Banks Group was employing 1,600 staff in 30 offices around the Asia Pacific region with revenues in excess of $450 million. Revenue for the year ended 31 Dec 1999 was $562 million.

Now based in New York, Andrew's out-of-hours interests include tennis, reading, movies, yoga and, lately, jogging in Central Park.

Notable for his success in a highly competitive industry Andrew credits fear of failure as a major motivator for himself and for most of the successful people he has interviewed. He believes that people who are driven by their passion and interest in their particular craft also hate the idea of failing or not being the best in their field. He doesn't see himself as being any different in that respect.

Enjoyment Factors

In the early days when I moved across from Human Resources some of my colleagues asked me whether I got bored interviewing people all day. I never really understood the question because I have never yet met two human beings the same and I am very curious about people.

It's great to be in a business in which we have a 'noble purpose'. We can build businesses and make good returns for shareholders by doing something very constructive – helping individuals achieve their career dreams and equipping organisations to do a much better job of attracting the talent they need to service their customers.

This is a pretty central issue in most people's lives because, after physical security, having food in your stomach and personal relationships, financial security and careers come next.

Inspirational People

The people who inspire me most have done something that is really unique. Something that demonstrates their willingness to take risks and break the boundaries. We only have one life (that we know of) and hiding behind the wall of safety seems a waste.

No 1 Recruitment Success Secret

As a recruiter I would like to think that during the interview process I uncovered uniqueness and greatness in people who have those qualities and then was able to convince them to try new career moves. This ability brought me success in placing non-traditional candidates in interesting roles.

No 1 Manager's Success Secret

Only hire the best and, by that I mean, the people with great values and quick minds. Next provide good processes and training to support them. Then get the hell out of their way.

Attributes of Top Recruiters

Some of the hallmarks of top recruiters would include:
- Having a genuine interest and curiosity about people, coupled with good intuitive abilities
- Being a good listener – the candidate should be doing 90 per cent of the talking
- Asking the client good questions and not talking too much during the sales process
- Having no fear of selling face-to-face or on the phone
- The ability to handle multiple transactions simultaneously at a fast pace
- And, looking to the near-future, they must be totally in love with the World Wide Web.

Advice to Recruiters Wanting To Be The Best

Always compete with yourself. This means keeping statistics on every aspect of what you do and analysing them each quarter. Irrespective of how well you've done you have to ask the question, 'how could I have done better'?

Advice to Owners & Managers Growing A Business

Hire the best people, train them and then accept that they probably have better ideas than you do so resist being a control freak.

In my experience the more equity we gave away to staff, through one scheme or another, the faster the company grew. Any recruitment firm that doesn't share the upside in success with its people has failed to recognise that it is a human capital management business. In that case it is failing to secure its most important asset.

Career Lessons Learned

In retrospect I wish I had started earlier – I was 30 before I got into the industry.

I would have taken Morgan & Banks into the IT/Telecommunications sector more quickly. With TMP we will be Number One in that space globally in the not too distant future but we could have got there faster if, in the early 90s, we hadn't been distracted by other opportunities.

The lessons learnt are too numerous to mention because, by virtue of our position, I think we have made more mistakes than most in the industry. If you grow a business like ours across so many markets and sectors, it's all about trying new things and hoping that 70 per cent of them take off.

Recruitment in 2005

The industry will be larger as a whole and, while there will be lower transaction value to the customer, the total volume of revenues will be up as much as 50 per cent.

This is because the Internet will bring more candidates and clients through the channel of intermediaries like us and make it less attractive for people to find their own jobs – this is still the biggest slice of the market.

Processes and reward systems will change dramatically. Any recruitment firm that can't offer clients more value-add than just knowing their local market and being competent will find their margins eroding.

To ensure future success the whole industry will need to be at the bleeding edge of understanding the Internet and its implications for recruiters – turning it to our advantage rather than seeing it as a threat.

Tony Beddison

Since 1977 Tony Beddison has held the position of Chairman of SACS Group, a sizeable diversified human resources organisation.

Part of his mandate with SACS Group has been to establish a value standard for dealing with clients, candidates and staff which has been reflected in the group's growth and performance.

Employing over 100 staff, SACS has aimed to attract and retain high calibre people who can share in the business and provide industry-leading service delivery that is driven by customer needs, not dollars.

Tony Beddison

Formerly a Lieutenant in the Australian Army, Tony is heavily involved in community service and public associations such as the Council of the Australian War Memorial, Chairman of Australia Day Committee, The Centenary of Federation Committee and Monash University Institute of Reproduction and Development Appeal.

He believes everyone should give part of their personal and financial resources back to the community in some way and estimates that he spends one day a week in community activities.

Motivation for Tony Beddison is linked to success and doing things well. As he says, "I want to play in the 1st XI – not the fourths. My personal esteem depends on excellence." For him it all comes back to wanting to win and be as successful as possible with well-defined goals.

Enjoyment Factors

This is an enjoyable industry in many ways. The dynamism of recruitment is important to my sense of satisfaction – every one of my 25 years has been different. It is a personal challenge to adapt to the changing market and community. Our service delivery and the usage of our service changes constantly – it's a dynamic, exciting, fast-moving industry.

Above all it is a people business. Not only do I enjoy working with my co-workers but it enormously satisfying to find a first-class solution to the needs of clients or candidates.

Inspirational People

Inspiration has come from many places over the years including all those people who built sizeable service companies from concept to implementation.

There are also inspirational individuals who have impressed me.

For example Jeff Kennett, former Victorian premier, was an inspiration because he demonstrated that you can not only change the way things are done in the community but also people's perceptions about themselves.
I find Bill Gates inspiring because he has proven there is no limit to intellectual capacity and service delivery. He shows how it is possible to build a business from nothing to the biggest in the world. There are others I could name but these are some examples of people I find inspiring.

No 1 Recruitment Success Secret

Recruiters, the secret of success is to really understand what your client is trying to achieve, not what you think they need. You can't be focused on making a fast placement.

No 1 Manager's Success Secret

Business owners and managers have to share with the people who are making it happen. Don't be greedy, share and care for your staff. Dismiss personal status and take pride in the people you work with.

Attributes of Top Recruiters

The best recruiters have these attributes:
- Integrity
- Intelligence
- Huge antenna – they are sensitive to what is being said and not being said
- A caring attitude
- Super-charged energy

They accept nothing but getting the right result for clients and candidates.

Advice to Recruiters Wanting To Be The Best

To be the best, a recruiter has to be prepared to put in the hard work. This is not a 9-5 business and there are no short cuts. You have to live it, breathe it, sleep it. You need a serious commitment to your career – you can't be an Olympic athlete without putting in the effort.

It's important to learn how to deliver top quality results. This industry requires constant learning and training – recruiters should invest in developing themselves. You must grow or get out because the market changes rapidly.

Take pride in everything you do so that you can walk down the street knowing that the people you meet, whether clients or candidates, respect you and had a positive experience dealing with your organisation. This only happens if you respect the dignity of everyone concerned without treating them impersonally, as a number or as just part of a process.

Advice to Owners & Managers Growing A Business

At the outset, you must have a consuming passion for the business to be successful.

Train, train, train. Spend lots of time on personal and professional development of all staff. Work on getting your internal human values right – value your people as they are the most important part of your business.

Management is an active thing. Keep track of your business with sophisticated reports and measurements e.g. weekly activity reports, detailed monthly financials. Also manage your debtors so that you get paid for your work. If you deliver a high quality service, it is reasonable to expect your client to fulfill their side of the contract and pay you on time. We must remember we are consultants not financiers.

Grow on profit, not on sales, because you can easily obtain volume but without profitability you won't be around for long.

Career Lessons Learned

Over my career I have learned a lot about people. Firstly, to work with consultants and managers that are high calibre and share your values and secondly, to recruit the highest quality individuals and reward them generously with shareholdings and financial returns.

In retrospect I would have given the people who contributed significantly to the business some ownership earlier rather than later. Also I would have been more ruthless on high performers who did not match our company values. There is no place in your organisation for prima donnas who will ride roughshod over your value set.

Recruitment in 2005

The industry will continue to grow with a decline in the do-it-yourself recruitment market. Companies will not do it themselves because they are not skilled – just as they do not run their own legal cases.

The industry will move increasingly into alliances and relationships with clients leading to a diminishing 'retail' market and entirely new ways of delivering service. The Internet will be a major factor in this, enabling us to reduce the cost of service. Clients will require faster and more flexible services, delivered primarily through the Internet. Recruitment organisations will need to add value to their client's business.

First Interview

One thing is certain. In 2005 we will not be doing things as we are today. As a result the industry must train its staff and continue to grow by providing sophisticated solutions. Firms should build on quality and not enter the business just to make money. Their reason for doing business should be to make a difference, for the long term, in the performance of client organisations.

Robert Blanche

Robert Blanche is co-owner of the Bayside Group of Companies, an Australian-owned corporation with an annual turnover of $90 million. He is Director of the Group's Recruitment Companies and Divisions which are located throughout Australia and employ 200 people.

Robert is proud of Bayside Group's relationships with staff including some extending back to the company's inception in 1976. His 25-year partnership with John Wilson and Ray Allen has withstood the test of time and continues to deepen.

Robert Blanche

Robert's pursuit of customer satisfaction has been vital in steering the growth of Bayside Personnel and other Group recruitment divisions.

His underlying commitment to achieving "best practice" in the industry culminates in his active participation with the RCSA. His various RCSA roles have encompassed President Victorian/Tasmanian Division, National Board member, National Treasurer and member of committees addressing OH&S and GST.

His interests include golf, racehorses, swimming, investment, cooking and parrot-breeding. He is immensely proud of the achievements of his three children who are of university age.

Robert believes that motivation is part of a person's makeup. He cites the example of footballers with average talent becoming champions because they are motivated. He modestly puts himself into that category of being averagely talented but extremely motivated. The desire to succeed and win has played a strong role throughout his working career and sporting activities.

Enjoyment Factors

When I first became involved in recruitment I enjoyed the challenge of the search for a candidate, the selection of the right candidate and the successful match between client and candidate. It was particularly rewarding when the candidate/client would demonstrate their appreciation.

On another level, I have greatly enjoyed my broader involvement in the industry as a whole through holding the position of RCSA President Victorian/Tasmanian Division and Treasurer of the RCSA Board. I believe the experiences, networking opportunities, relationships and knowledge I gained helped me to become a far better person.

I have a very strong commitment to seeing the recruitment and consulting profession maintain the highest possible level of professional and ethical values. I have found this experience over the last six years to be very rewarding.

Inspirational People

I find it easy to relate to people who have shown tenacity, endurance and competence and end up achieving great things. If there were one person to look up to in recent times it would have to be President Nelson Mandela.

I have seen a number of these qualities within industry colleagues who have run successful businesses and yet have given so much back to this industry.

The list is long and I think it would be inappropriate to mention names as I may leave someone out.

No 1 Recruitment Success Secret

There is no doubt in my mind that the three competencies at the top of the tree are persistence and motivation, along with the desire to win. All other competencies and skills will develop under those attributes.

No 1 Manager's Success Secret

In addition to persistence and motivation, integrity is essential if you are to be in business for any length of time. It is important to have a long-term view on all business relationships particularly those of your customers, staff, candidates and industry colleagues. Many business owners/managers do not see their staff, customers and candidates as stakeholders and consequently do not reap the full benefits that may be available to them.

Attributes of Top Recruiters

- Persistence
- Motivation
- Sense of urgency
- Good interpersonal/communication skills
- A desire to continually develop.

Advice to Recruiters Wanting To Be The Best

The recruiter needs to ask him or herself, 'Am I just giving this statement lip service or do I really want to be the best?' Those who wish to be the best will continually thirst for knowledge, study the business sections of newspapers, read all industry-related material/magazines, keep abreast of legislation, participate in industry associations, be prepared to give their time freely for gains in the future and not be money driven. These people will see their future being determined by their past.

Advice to Owners & Managers Growing A Business

From my own experience the greatest advice I could offer any owner or manager would be to clearly identify when the time has come to let go of the hands-on activities and become a manager. If clear direction strategies and plans are in place, and not shared with all stakeholders, there is a good chance the company will end up on the road to nowhere.

Secondly, a good manager must recognise that the staff is an asset. Giving them the opportunity to develop and grow within the organisation and their chosen career is an excellent investment.

Career Lessons Learned

When I first started in business I did not identify the importance of creating a career path for staff and providing them with the facilities to reach their goals.

I would have set in place methods of measuring customer and staff satisfaction, finances and trends, giving a greater importance to evaluating risk in my various enterprises and activities at the beginning of my business operations.

1990 was a year when many personnel companies went out of business, for a variety of reasons. We set in place a business strategy to diversify the group's activities to cover any downturn in any part of the industry. 1990 was one of the Bayside Group's most successful years. This illustrated a great lesson for any business, 'Make sure you can manage the major risks if you want to survive'.

Recruitment in 2005

Of the top 100 companies listed under the Standard & Poors index in 1980, 75 per cent are no longer listed because they have either gone broke or changed their business activities. By the time the year 2005 comes around there is no doubt there will be significant change to the recruitment industry particularly with the introduction of technology, the pressure of unions and society.

We can compare this industry to the architectural, engineering and accounting sectors; pressures on fees have had a significant impact on the viability of those industries and it would be reasonable to assume this will apply to recruitment. We are already seeing significant signs of this occurring. When fees are under pressure any significant downturn will result in many companies struggling to survive and that's often when ethical values deteriorate.

For this industry to survive it is essential that companies implement risk management programs to avert any significant risk to their business.

Nanette Carroll

Nan Carroll has been Joint Managing Director of Alectus Personnel, the Office Services Division of Morgan and Banks, since April 2000. Before that, she was Joint Managing Director of Brook Street Recruitment with Kathryn Devine.

Having Kathryn as a business partner has been an important part of Nan's success. Together they led the company from a 10-person entity of $1.5 million turnover in 1990, following a management buyout, to $23 million in 1999 supporting 32 staff. They then negotiated the sale of Brook Street Recruitment to TMP Worldwide in August 1999.

Nanette Carroll

Nan's start in recruitment came when she joined Slade Consulting Group in 1981. However, her first position was not as a consultant but as office manager to Andrew Banks.

While raising three small children alone, she moved into consulting after only three months and worked her way up through the ranks. With no formal training, at that time, she was thrilled that her first placement lasted for seven years.

She became Queensland Manager in 1983, National Sales and Marketing Manager in 1986 and Regional Director in 1987. Ultimately, she took on a board position at Brook Street Bureau (UK Company) in 1988.

Relaxation is now an important part of her life. Nan loves walking, reading, swimming and entertaining, often at her beach apartment in Currumbin, Queensland with Mike, her husband since 1985, who has been a very strong supporter of her professional life.

At first, Nan's motivation was pure survival. Single-handedly raising three children under five years of age meant her priorities were to put food on the table and keep body, mind, and soul together.

She talks of inheriting a strong work ethic from her parents who led by example. Nan's father taught her to work for things rather than wait to be given them. It is a lesson she has put into practice throughout her career.

Enjoyment Factors

I am challenged by this industry every single day. I enjoy the constant change of today's market and having to find innovative ways of doing things. People are demanding results immediately – it is exciting trying to meet client and candidate expectations and every person you touch has a different need.

I love seeing people achieve – watching staff blossom with confidence and success. It is one of the most fantastic experiences seeing the possibilities in people and helping them reach a potential they may not have even seen in themselves.

Inspirational People

Andrew Banks inspired me. From the very early days, he had the passion, vision, and charisma. He drove me to believe in myself and succeed when, at that stage, I did not have confidence in myself. Andrew gave me fantastic skills right up front – he took the fear out of me.

Geoff Slade saw my potential and offered me opportunities and challenges ahead of where I thought I could be. Like Andrew he could see the promise and would not let me say no to new promotions within the company.

My father had a saying, 'You have to get up in the morning, look in the mirror and like whom you see. If you do that – you can do anything!'

No 1 Recruitment Success Secret

Never forget that people are important. Do something with every candidate you bring into the office – under-promise and over-deliver to both clients and candidates.

No 1 Manager's Success Secret

Always have a strategic plan and stick to it. This has been our single most important success factor in growing Brook Street Recruitment.

Attributes of Top Recruiters

To be a top recruiter you need to:
• Be a great listener
• Inspire trust in your knowledge and ability
• Treat others with respect
• Pay attention to detail
• Work with clients who will treat your placements well and, most importantly,
• Keep your ego under control.

Advice to Recruiters Wanting To Be The Best

Take the time to really develop your business and commercial acumen. Read finance and business journals to 'talk the talk' with clients. This business is all about trust – clients must feel certain that they can trust your judgement.

I cannot emphasise respect enough. Do not forget – today's candidate is tomorrow's client. Your own good name is critical, even in the early days, and your actions can severely impact on the reputation of you and your organisation.

Do not skimp on the details just to make the placement because this will shoot you in the foot every time. This business is not rocket science – it is just about good common sense.

Retain the human touch – candidates are gold, especially in today's market! If you do things right everyone benefits – candidates, clients and you! Work smarter, not harder, with focus on working well with a loyal group of clients.

Advice to Owners & Managers – Growing A Business

Hire the best people and look after them very well, not just with money – be committed to developing their career. Training from day one is critical and must be followed with ongoing training – people want constant learning and development. The reason most people leave a company is because they do not know their next step. Performance appraisal and career development is vital.

Do what you say you will do. Be up front with expectations and key performance indicators and make sure you do not move the goal posts. Don't leave any surprises for your staff to guess at. Tell them the good, the bad, and the ugly news.

Don't try to do business with the whole world. Instead, create strong partnerships with a select group of clients.

Your five-year strategic plan is critical. Review it every month and constantly communicate your plans and vision to your staff. Know the productivity of your people so you can help them achieve even more than they think possible. Know the hot buttons of your people – so you can retain them. Find out what motivates them, whether it be money, life balance, career path or education.

Accurate monthly reporting should be your Bible. Regular formal meetings where you sit and analyse will give you very in-depth knowledge of your business upon which to base future actions and plans.

Know your cash flow and get your pricing right. You must know how much it costs to be in business and what you need to run the business. The industry is allowing clients to force prices down. If you do not know how much it costs to run your business then you could be in big trouble.

If discounting, it must be win-win for both parties. Heavy discounting can erode the quality of service you are delivering. We must have faith and confidence in the job we do. Recruitment is not about price – it is about quality.

Career Lessons Learned

I prefer to look forward and not back. However in the early days I had very little balance in my life and drove myself too hard. I was always trying to be the best mother and the best manager without looking after myself. It got so bad that I once blacked out while driving on the freeway. Fortunately the car was stationary at the time. The doctors said my bucket was full!

We need to be efficient and have balance in our life. We are very conscious of a 'family friendly' policy now, with modems for people to work from home, and flexible working hours for staff. This means we have been able to encourage tremendous staff loyalty.

In the early days, I learned you must give people two clear parameters from the very beginning. We were a bit ad hoc at the start but quickly learned that staff need focus and direction.

We were trying to be all things to all people. We were unable to say no and then we ended up being over-committed – we did learn!

Recruitment in 2005

The world is getting smaller. We are now part of a global market. We need to be an 'employer of choice' to attract the right people. Our recruitment firms need to have credibility, professionalism, and a good social conscience.

The war for talent will get tougher. Severe candidate shortages will continue, because three years is now the average time spent at a company and recruitment firms must provide even more candidates to meet the demand.

The Internet will play an enormous part in ensuring we capture every resume. For example, our Internet recruitment site, monster.com now has 2 million resumes and, within two years, will have 31 million. The whole focus is on capturing people when they leave school and developing their careers throughout their lives.

There will be more e-solutions. We will be a very technology-based industry. However, with all this drive towards new technology and with the industry's changes over the last 20 years it is still about relationships, and treating people well.

Malcolm Jackman

Malcolm Jackman joined Manpower Australia/New Zealand in 1996 with the aim of expanding the company. As Chief Executive he oversees the company's 500 staff based in over 90 offices.

A current annual turnover in excess of $400 million signals a major leap from the 1995 figures of $20 million.

A highlight of his time at Manpower is the Australian Defence Force permanent recruitment contract finalised in June 2000 under which the company will recruit up to 10,000 people a year.

Malcolm Jackman

New Zealand-born Malcolm studied mathematics and accounting before joining the Royal New Zealand Navy and then embarking on a career in staff services.

He has worked with organisations such as Slade Consulting Group in Auckland and spent seven years with Adia (now Adecco) in senior roles in New Zealand, USA and Australia.

Now based in Sydney, Malcolm has dual Australian and New Zealand citizenship. With his wife and three teenage sons, he enjoys boating on Sydney Harbour as well as modern impressionist art, Rugby Union and golf.

According to Malcolm he is driven by the hunger to keep succeeding – he never allows himself to be satisfied with just today. This ongoing quest is based in the knowledge that the money is nice but it's better to be good; the best; the most successful person.

His strong inner motivation has sometimes led to the suggestion that he has a big ego. He concedes that this may be the case but sees it more as an unerring confidence in his own ability to succeed. He will not rest until Manpower is Number One in Australia and New Zealand.

Enjoyment Factors

I just love the people in the business; they are intelligent, extroverted and dynamic. Competitors are a joy to be with, especially at the bar.

The industry by nature is transactional so you get constant wins – placing permanents and temps. You are always achieving things.

The other great part of the job is the diversity of our client's business. I couldn't be a specialist recruiter – I want to be in a bank one day and a factory the next.

Inspirational People

Within the industry there are several people who have significantly influenced me.

Mitchell Fromstein, Manpower's former Chairman, has an unbelievably visionary brain. Every time he talks (even now at 70) he is inspirational. His ability to see the future put fire in my belly – when you can see the end it is so easy to keep going.

I also admire John Bowmer, CEO Adecco Worldwide, having worked with him over a long period of time. He taught me lots about 'hard-arse' management and how to run a business well.

Within Australia I like and admire Geoff Slade, one of the great characters of the industry. He continues to devote his life to the industry. Another great character is John Plummer Snr. who has tremendous business acumen.

No 1 Recruitment Success Secret

Two things:
- Control all parts of the process – never give up control to the client or candidate. This is what they are paying you to do. If you give them control they won't know what to do with it.
- Closure at every step of the way. Close, close, close. A series of closes along the way will collectively make the placement.

No 1 Manager's Success Secret

Running a business is a matter of solving a simple mathematical equation: sales minus expenses equals profit.

Any fool can measure profit and even the dullest manager can control costs – it is selling that is most important. The real key to success is focusing on sales. Most people in business don't want to be salespeople and that's why most people don't get to be the boss. Although we have an exceptionally talented director of sales I am still the chief sales officer as well as CEO.

Attributes of Top Recruiters

You must have the ability to see the big picture as well as take care of the detail – the follow-up and return phone calls. If I could pick the one word that describes a great recruiter it would be 'detail'.

Huge personality and intelligence are not enough. Even people with modest personality and intelligence can be great recruiters if they focus on detail.

Advice to Recruiters Wanting To Be The Best

Being a recruiter is like mowing lawns. You don't mow the lawn, you just push the lawn mower. So you are never going to place anyone in a job.

The candidate is the one who will get the job. Your job as a recruiter is to get the right candidate in front of the right client for the right job. If you think this way you will be a great recruiter. A great recruiter is the facilitator of the recruitment process, not the decision maker.

Advice to Owners & Managers Growing A Business

Without doubt spend your time in the business and not on the business. This is where you make the money. That's it – the easiest and most simple piece of advice I can give you.

Career Lessons Learned

Off the top of my head I'd say I should have been less of a party animal at conferences!

But seriously there are not many things I would have done differently. I would have liked to be CEO of Manpower 20 years ago, but I wasn't capable then. All my stuff-ups have made me successful today because I have learned from them. This is perhaps why I am at the top because I made mistakes and learned from them. A bit like Babe Ruth, the greatest baseball player of his era, who scored more home runs than anyone else but also struck out the most.

I don't want to own and run my own business because I made that mistake and I learned it was something I didn't want to do. I am completely fulfilled by being a corporate warrior and not a business owner.

Recruitment in 2005

The industry will not be significantly different to the way it is now, as businesses are not being rationalised as predicted.

There will continue to be businesses of all sizes and shapes. However I hope that we will see a much greater penetration by the industry into the small- and medium- sized business sector. If this doesn't happen then significant rationalisation could occur.

The industry will continue to grow dramatically, at a minimum of 15 per cent per annum because all the reasons which fuel growth today, such as outsourcing and business expansion in general, will continue to be important factors in the next few years.

Dorothy Jellett

Dorothy Jellett is Managing Director of Melbourne-based DFP Recruitment Services which also trades as Dorothy Farmer Personnel. Dorothy purchased the business in 1986 with a headcount of five people and now employs 50, with a turnover in excess of $20 million.

She is also Director of a Sydney recruitment services business and is about to add a Brisbane branch to the operation. Through her innovative leadership DFP has become an industry-leader particularly in the provision of temporary and permanent office-based staff.

Dorothy Jellet

In 1988 Dorothy introduced the Australian market to the QWIZ software testing program for office staff which has since become an industry standard. In 1992, with the proposed introduction of the Superannuation Guarantee Legislation, she saw and acted on the opportunity for the industry body to develop a national superannuation fund to cater for the needs of temporary staff and members' employees.

Dorothy was recognised by her staff through a nomination for the Inaugural Telstra Business Women's Awards in 1995 and was a finalist in the Victorian Small Business Owner category.

Prior to DFP, Dorothy worked with Chandler & Macleod Consultants in Melbourne from 1972 to 1986, initially as a temporary staff consultant, moving through various operating roles and taking on management responsibility as each opportunity presented itself. As General Manager of the Melbourne City office she worked to build a culture of success, staff stability and professionalism, achieving a turnover of $9 million with a staff of 28.

Although work is a major interest Dorothy is also involved in outside committees and boards. She has regularly worked on industry, government and employer association committees. When she gets the chance she likes to escape to her family's house at Nelson Bay and apartment on the golf course at Cape Schanck.

Dorothy considers herself to have been a 'late-starter' in commencing her own business. The desire to prove that she could do it was a prime motivator. She has enjoyed the fruits of her labour and the experience of financial success.

The eldest of five children, she grew up in country Victoria and New South Wales, where her hardworking parents instilled in her a strong work ethic. At just 16 she was in the workforce in a secretarial role and has never looked back.

A quietly persistent optimist, Dorothy has a strong will to succeed though never at the expense of other people. She tends to run on adrenaline and embraces the challenges posed by the business world.

Enjoyment Factors

It has been great to see the industry come of age and, as time has progressed, I have enjoyed it more. Having been in the industry 28 years, I have seen it grow and develop to become an important and valuable service to business as well as to people seeking employment. It is a dynamic industry – closely attuned to changes in the business world and the economy. And now we are experiencing the benefits and challenge of Web-based technology.

I applaud the open discussion and self-regulation of the industry. Recruiters today are sharing information and have more camaraderie, which pleases me. I believe the industry is finally recognised now as a peer to any other professional business service provider.

The industry's peak body, the RCSA, is providing education for people in the industry and addresses recruiting issues through national and state committees. United we go forward, but divided, we can't hope to influence the change that is necessary to guarantee our future.

The thing I don't like is the trend towards commoditising the procurement of recruitment services based solely on price. Our role is to 'provide quality human beings to work with quality human beings'. Our candidates have valuable and individual skill sets – in fact we're ultimately judged by the quality of match of these skills and the person's ability to fit into our client's culture. We can, and do, add value. Price should be just one factor when companies select a service provider.

Inspirational People

My first job in people management was as Staff Officer reporting to Jim Goulstone, a Director of advertising agency, USP Benson. He taught me to take responsibility for things but he also backed me regardless of the outcome. I responded by having the confidence to take on more senior responsibilities. My farewell card said, "To Dorothy, who makes personnel personal."

Doug Macleod, psychologist and co-founder of Chandler & Macleod, was another important influence. He showed confidence in me both as an HR professional and a manager in my early days at C&M. As a referee for me in the mid-1970s for part-time studies he also acknowledged my potential. So it was then up to me to deliver!

I wouldn't have achieved what I have without my parents and husband. My parents were an inspiration because of the value system, work ethic and underlying self-reliance they imparted to me. It is a bit sad they don't know all their children have been operating successful businesses for some years.

My husband has inspired me by being very supportive, providing me with stability, encouragement and acting as a sounding board while I developed my career. His support was essential to me when I was taking the risk to acquire Dorothy Farmer Personnel and grew it to become the business it is today.

No 1 Recruitment Success Secret

Be persistent. Listen and respond to other people's needs. Never stop learning.

Remember the old adage – 'do unto others...'

Today's candidate may well be tomorrow's client. Anyone you meet can appear at later stages of your life and in any part of the world, as I've found. So treat everyone in a professional responsive manner. The trail you leave behind becomes your reputation – try to make sure it's one you are proud of.

No 1 Manager's Success Secret

Although as the business owner I facilitate policy, finances and direction, I could not have built a business without supporting the learning and development of my staff. As a manager you must know that you can't do it by yourself. Trust your people and be supportive of them because they are the ones who will grow the business. Create an environment in which they can succeed and grow – as individuals and as part of a team. Look after their emotional health to gain maximum commitment. Develop family-friendly policies.

Communication and accepting feedback is also important. Owners should also be tuned into the external environment to anticipate and respond rapidly to change.

Attributes of Top Recruiters

A top recruiter needs:
• Credibility
• Business acumen
• Intuition
• Persistence
• Knowledge
• Ability to work under pressure
• Customer focus.

Advice to Recruiters Wanting To Be The Best

Make a firm commitment to your career. Focus on the assignment and your goals and those of your employer. Keep learning. Don't give up. Take a risk when you need to.

Adopt a creative approach to problem-solving. Accept responsibility and find a solution. Be challenged. Be someone your clients and candidates can trust.

Advice to Owners & Managers Growing A Business

Owning and managing a business will offer ongoing and constant challenges. Choose and coach your people well. Keep tuned into the business, its systems, people and future direction. Create a culture in which people want to work.

Plan ahead but also be aware of the changing external environment – move with it. Try to anticipate the future needs of your business, your clients, your candidates and your staff.

As a manager you're acting on behalf of the shareholder and owners of the business so respond to their objectives. As an owner you have to live with your own decisions – the good and the not-so-good.

You also have responsibility for funding your business so the relationship with your financier is important. You take on the business risk and it can be a very satisfying experience. But it's also a challenge and can be scary at times. Just remember to seek advice, it's not a weakness.

Career Lessons Learned

An awareness that nothing is really new – although it's often been a 'first' for me. I've learned by experience, as well as to seek counsel when it's needed.

It is important to keep abreast of the big picture which helps us to understand how we must craft and adapt our business strategy.

I've enjoyed taking responsibility and giving something back to the industry that has been good to me. There are always opportunities to get involved. Sometimes it's difficult to say no. But it's good to know that your participation on a committee or involvement in an activity will benefit both your business and our industry. It can be satisfying to know you've contributed to something that makes a difference out there.

Recruitment in 2005

In 2005, e-commerce technology will be old hat for recruitment service companies, with Business-to-Business on-line communication and transactions the norm. The industry will need to have developed a solution-based approach and offer value added services to clients, candidates and the company's own employees to remain viable.

New skill sets will have emerged, others will have disappeared. Although it's not possible to accurately predict the future we can be sure that the current speed of change will continue. This will offer new opportunities and a major shift in how we manage and access databases generally – both for the office and in our daily lives.

Our industry will be even more globalised by 2005, but niche players who link with others to share technology can also expect to play a role in local markets. The niche approach will continue to be a viable alternative to a multi-national service provider.

Would I do it all again? Most certainly, although it's going to be even more complex and challenging in tomorrow's business environment.

Graham Jenkins

Graham Jenkins has been Managing Director of Trinity Group since January 1992. With fellow director Wayne Simpson, he now oversees a staff of 26 people and an annual turnover of $7 million.

Trinity has enjoyed profitable growth each year since he bought the business in 1991 when there were just two employees. The company is organised into four divisions servicing Sales & Marketing, IT&T, Property & Engineering and Office Support/Administration.

Graham Jenkins

Prior to joining Trinity Group Graham spent four years with Morgan & Banks as a consultant and before this worked in marketing and general management roles with multi-national companies in Britain and Australia.

He sees his career path as comprising a number of small steps or building blocks, starting from running his own research business at the age of 19 while still at university.

Originally from the suburbs of London, UK, Graham now enjoys a Balmain lifestyle and counts cinema, current affairs, keeping fit and family activities among his leisure interests.

He is proud of his wife's own successful market research career and considers that his two children are lovely people with good solid values and promising futures. Another major achievement has been the experience of growing the team at Trinity Group and helping to bring new opportunities to so many people over the years.

According to Graham he is competitive with a well-defined desire to win, and has been for as long as he can remember. At school, he combined a desire to be popular with what he describes as a dismal lack of talent on the sporting field. Instead he worked hard to be academically popular with teachers and socially popular with his peers.

He recalls his regular study habits that saw him going to bed long after his parents each night. And all just to satisfy his inner competitive instincts.

Enjoyment Factors

In this very progressive industry no day is the same. Done well, recruitment is a complicated job that sees you dealing with both candidates and clients who don't always express their needs and feelings clearly.

I enjoy solving problems in a creative way. Spotting a candidate's true potential and using the search process to open someone's eyes to new possibilities. Winning over a client or a candidate with a convincing argument. At the end of the day there are winners and losers in the industry and you always know where you stand. The industry really appeals to my competitive nature.

I also like the chance to give people new opportunities. I am inspired by the way Trinity Group's good work can change people's lives. Not just of candidates but also of clients – because when we find them key staff we can make their businesses stronger.

Inspirational People

As a teenager I worked for a sales manager selling magazines. He told me to make sure I knocked on every door because 'the one you don't canvass is the one that would have bought from you'. That thought always seems to pop into my mind when I have a pile of prospects or resumes in front of me and keeps me going until I find what I need.

In the recruitment industry, Geoff Morgan and Andrew Banks were my main inspiration. I joined them in the mid 1980s shortly after they set up Morgan & Banks. They had recruited for years but were still very hands-on. They were meticulous and really cared about their work, their clients and their candidates. Their interview notes were always exactly what good interview notes should be. Together Geoff and Andrew changed the face of executive recruitment in this country by raising standards to a whole new level.

No 1 Recruitment Success Secret

Build a good candidate database. This means interviewing as many people as possible in your specialist industry sector. Learn how to interview well and know everything you can about successful people in your specialist field.

No 1 Manager's Success Secret

The first objective in a business is to survive so it is critical to manage the cash so you can pay for the services you are delivering. Find good people, motivate them, keep them and manage your cash flow.

Any business is only successful if the people in it know how to do a good job. Recruiting and training those good people enables you to consistently deliver high service levels.

Attributes of Top Recruiters

Drive – Because good recruitment is hard work. Both clients and candidates have expectations and top recruiters are prepared to work at a pace which meets those expectations.

Intelligence – You are bombarded with problems to solve every single day and you need intelligence to define and solve those problems quickly and effectively.

Integrity – Do what you say you will and live by a set of values and principles.

Intuition – 50 per cent of the time you are told the whole truth but 50 per cent of the time you have to work it out for yourself. Your intuition tells you what not to take at face value. Combine all the information in front of you with your intuition to form a conclusion.

Persuasiveness – You must be able to persuade a client to follow a strategy you think will solve their problem, and persuade a candidate to consider various options. If you can't present an argument clearly and logically, you won't succeed in executive recruitment.

Advice to Recruiters Wanting To Be The Best

There are lots of ways to be successful in recruitment. Read and learn from other recruiters and find a way that works with your personal style.

You can become the best recruiter of blue-collar staff or the best recruiter of bankers but you shouldn't try to become both. Find the segment of the industry in which you want to be the best and work at it.

Advice to Owners & Managers Growing A Business

To build a great company the business needs a sense of progress. You need a clear plan, leadership and a sense of direction. You must listen to the ideas of your staff, clients and candidates.

Use some of your profit to invest in training, technology and marketing. Add people with new skills. Share your strategy with your team. Make sure you follow business principles with a well-defined marketing plan, revenue and profit targets.

Don't become too emotionally attached to the business – this might stop you from cutting costs when you should.

Career Lessons Learned

In the early part of my career I took it all way too seriously. Today I find it easier not to get so upset when things don't go according to plan.

In hindsight I would probably have studied for an MBA to update my formal learning and help develop my business problem-solving skills.

At Trinity Group I believe we should have established team managers at an earlier stage. This would have allowed us to grow faster and develop people more rapidly.

First Interview

Recruitment in 2005

In many ways it will be much the same, interviewing candidates just as we have been doing for thirty years. Basic processes like that will survive although the approach will be more rigorous and disciplined.

But we will certainly see technology and databases speed up the process with fewer candidate interviews. I see different groups of recruiters acting virtually as a data warehouse of candidates, and other groups adding more value to both client and candidate through advanced processes and taking more time to understand needs.

The most successful Internet job-sites will probably specialise in particular disciplines.

I see the industry continuing to become more professional and worthy as a long-term career for human resource graduates. I hope our industry will progressively develop more confidence in itself to win more respect from HR managers. It will help dispel the problem of HR managers complaining about poor service whilst wanting low prices. Recruitment firms need to educate HR managers about the relationship between price and value and not automatically bow to price pressure.

The industry must ensure recruitment standards are raised through education and training, and by paying consultants competitive salaries and performance-linked bonuses rather than mainly commission. This change will shift the approach away from what some people see as selling a resume to more professional recruitment that meets the needs of both candidate and client.

Reg Maxwell

Formerly Managing Director of Allstaff, Reg Maxwell's career is a testament to his dedication and determination to stay in business – no matter what.

For the past seven years he has been a sought-after consultant specialising in Quality Management for the recruitment industry. He developed and delivered a QA training program for recruitment consultancies, with over 300 pages of supporting material. This included samples of all necessary documentation for a recruitment firm to obtain Quality Endorsement plus consulting support.

Reg Maxwell

Having set up his first business as a licensed insurance broker in Brisbane in 1964, Reg established Allstaff in 1966 to find employees for the local insurance sector. In 1967 Reg sold his interest in the brokerage to concentrate on Allstaff which was the first full-time dedicated recruiting business in Queensland.

By 1973, Allstaff had expanded to become one of the larger firms on the eastern seaboard with 25 staff and a Head Office in Brisbane CBD, two others in the suburbs and plans for two more offices within the following 18 months. However it was a turbulent time and the business was affected by a number of factors.

With the once-in-50-years Australia Day floods of January 1974 much of Brisbane was underwater for up to nine days. Many businesses simply never reopened but Allstaff survived, winding back to five staff and only one office. The worst recession in many years hit in February 1973, job orders slowed to a trickle and 673 of Allstaff's former clients were not listed in the next published phone book. Another 400 were in desperate situations and remained dormant clients for another four years.

Reg decided to rebuild the business with a new focus on larger CBD accounts which meant winning them away from other providers. Allstaff was one of the first recruitment operations to use computer technology, as early as 1982. In 1985 Reg started an executive relocation business called Relocating Queensland, servicing the oil and mining companies. In 1986 he added a Nursing Agency and his staff was back up to a headcount of 20.

1990 saw the sale of Allstaff to Western Personal and Reg managed the combined Queensland operation until 1992. Having introduced Quality Management to Allstaff prior to the sale Reg was retained as a consultant to complete the job. Allstaff-Western received certification in 1993 making it the first in the recruitment industry to be endorsed by the Quality Assurance Services.

Reg was one of four founding member of Queensland's first industry association in July 1969 and held every executive office including being elected President seven times. He was the Queensland representative on the National Body for over 20 years and National President from 1992-94.

His first interest now is to spend time with his wife and children. He is a keen reader of history and novels, is a hopeful gardener rather than a good one, and a would-be sailor of small boats if he had the time. He also enjoys the theatre and concerts.

Like many early entrants into the industry Reg just fell into recruitment and found that, once he was working for himself, it was hard to work for someone else. The drive to 'keep doing his own thing' was a strong motivator.

First Interview

He was motivated by the mental challenge and stimulation of running a business and could not imagine doing anything else. For him it is important to see things through, using his skills and knowledge to just keep going.

Enjoyment Factors

The industry was young and always changing and I liked that. It was a real challenge to promote recruitment as a professional industry.

I really enjoyed running a business and the relationships I built with clients both as a recruiter and as a manager/consultant were a source of great satisfaction. I also enjoyed the relationships with the people who worked with me – we had a harmonious team and we worked well together.

Inspirational People

Many people in the early years gave me guidance.

The late George Carter, who worked in the Queensland insurance business, taught me about service, dealing with clients and making the most of your time to give the best level of service.

Another manager in the insurance business taught me money management and cost control, inspiring me to study accounting.

John Plummer did an enormous amount of work for the recruitment industry in Australia. He was unstinting in his support for both industry bodies (NAPC and IPC), giving his own time and encouraging his staff to be involved. He also built the biggest of the Australian-owned businesses, with branches in New Zealand and London.

Another man who did a tremendous amount of work for the industry is John McArthur. He was President of the NAPC when the IPC was launched and I know that he virtually took six months away from his business to get it started, travelling all over Australia to persuade people of the need to get behind it.

Joan May, of Premium Personnel in Sydney, was the first President of the IPC and she gave a great deal of her time to ensuring it had good operating systems and worthwhile course material. Without her input it is doubtful it would have been as successful as it was.

No 1 Recruitment Success Secret

Service to the client. The role is to look after the client – they are the reason you are in the business and being successful.

The candidate is a close second – be honest with them and treat them with care. I work on the principle of 'doing as you would be done by'.

No 1 Manager's Success Secret

If you can manage people and manage money then you can run a business. You need to keep your people so it's essential to have good efficient systems and a support administrative structure that works for them.

Attributes of Top Recruiters

Recruiters need these attributes to be the best:
• Persistence and determination
• Analytical mind
• Objectiveness
• Being prepared to give the best possible service.

The ability to make money doesn't hurt, as it is essential to the business if managed correctly.

Intelligence is important and, today, formal qualifications are a must. Clients expect to deal with professionally qualified people.

Advice to Recruiters Wanting To Be The Best

Do everything you can to build the qualities mentioned above. Study courses at the RCSA or AHRI.

Remember persistence and determination is the name of the game – so whatever happens, just keep going.

Don't work in isolation but when you enter the industry, join a professional organisation and learn how to work with your peers.

Advice to Owners & Managers Growing A Business

Growing a recruitment business is just like any other enterprise. It takes lots of dedication and puts a strain on personal relationships – be sure you are ready for this.

One of the most dangerous times is when you are in transitional growth. This is the time to seek outside professional consultants, especially growing from small to medium or from medium to large.

Career Lessons Learned

There are some things I would have done with different timing. I would have decided earlier to appoint non-executive directors on to the board in order to give discipline to set budgets and also to get independent input and another perspective.

I would have expanded into the larger Sydney and Melbourne markets sooner. In 1972 Allstaff had the opportunity and resources to replicate its success in other cities. However, at the time this was a lifestyle decision so I don't regret making it.

Recruitment in 2005

Technology is changing everything. The Internet will have an increasing impact and, to be honest, I don't know how the industry will develop. The big may get bigger and medium-sized companies might disappear. This extrapolates the current trend towards being larger or specialising. Technology will have a significant impact.

The industry needs to continue becoming more professional so that it receives the recognition given to other professions.

The industry needs a national voice and should support the RCSA as a vehicle to do this. We need a central group of spokespeople where the media can go to ask for comment – the way the AMA is positioned in the medical sector. To this end I think the RCSA needs more support from the industry and perhaps a marketing campaign to lift its profile even further.

Geoff Moles

As an 'A' grade squash player and golfer with a handicap of 15, Geoff Moles is in a good position to demonstrate a personal ambition to succeed.

Geoff had been managing IT software house, Datec, when he established Candle in March 1984 with the view of starting his own software house. He saw the immediate demand for IT contractors and developed a recruitment business that would cater to the contract and permanent recruitment needs of a range of clients.

Geoff Moles

From an initial headcount of three he expanded the business through organic growth and acquisition. Candle purchased Melbourne and Brisbane-based Data Personnel in November 1996.

Candle listed on the ASX on 16 January 1997 with a capitalisation of $25.5 million which led to the company's acquisition of other IT recruitment companies, Doughty Group, New Zealand's largest IT recruiter, in November 1997 and Unisys People in December 1999.

In March 1999 Candle embarked on the strategy to become a full service recruiter with the acquisition of Freeman Adams, a specialist in Banking and Finance recruitment. Freeman Adams has since expanded into Accounting and Office Support recruitment.

Candle now has 280 employees in Australia and New Zealand and is on track to turn over in excess of $200 million in 2000.

As well as being driven by personal ambition Geoff, a father of four teenagers, is motivated by the satisfaction of growing a business and the experience of seeing his staff grow and be successful along with it.

The competitive nature of the business provides a great environment for personal growth and development and he says he has learned a lot from the opportunities and challenges of running a public company.

Enjoyment Factors

Growth is at the heart of what I enjoy most about this business. We have expanded the company through establishing new offices like the one we have just opened in Christchurch, New Zealand. It is also exciting to take the business into new spheres of recruitment such as banking, accounting and office support.

I'm grateful of having the opportunity to watch staff develop. It really enhances our ability to keep finding and providing the best people as both staff and contractors for our clients. When you do things right there is also the chance to see the share price grow which is very enjoyable.

Inspirational People

Of the many people who have had an influence on me a few stand out as being inspirational at key times in my career.

Andrew Banks and Geoff Morgan were an inspiration for me to grow the business and go public with Candle.

Harry Douglas and Brian Lees who ran Datec helped me to understand how to run a professional services organisation and opened my eyes to the opportunities in the services industry in Australia.

No 1 Recruitment Success Secret

A good recruiter requires the ability to focus on the task – while keeping control of thousands of balls in the air at any one time. The most important factors are to manage recruitment activity as a whole, keeping an eye on the big picture, while developing and maintaining good relationships with clients and candidates.

No 1 Manager's Success Secret

There is no doubt in my mind that selecting quality people is fundamental to success. It is essential to manage the business environment as it grows, guided by a well-developed strategy that considers the business opportunities with clients and future growth opportunities.

Attributes of Top Recruiters

Many of the characteristics of top recruiters are the attributes that would suit any manager in a professional services environment.

- Focus
- High Energy
- Excellent people selection skills – matching client culture with candidate ability
- Ambition
- Good people relationship skills
- Ability to run teams with good management skills
- Integrity and honesty
- Sales Ability.

Advice to Recruiters Wanting To Be The Best

The way to maintain control of the many parts of a dynamic business is to know the secret: to do a little bit of everything, everyday. Everything from telephone calls and prospecting for new business to filling client assignments.

The other secret is to never rest on your laurels but to keep working on the skills you need for successful recruitment, new business development and people management.

Use Key Performance Indicators (KPIs) to monitor your activity, reach targets and make placements. Recruitment is all about numbers – meeting your KPIs will give you a much better chance of success.

Advice to Owners & Managers Growing A Business

Do things from a position of strength. By that I mean don't open an office in Canberra if you only have the management depth and funding necessary for three months instead of 12 months. If you take on a new client or consultant ensure you have the financial and management capability to commit to following through with the required support and infrastructure. Diversify your client base to reduce your reliance on single clients.

You must be patient with growth and avoid stretching yourself or the business by being too ambitious. Owners should not overcommit themselves personally with big boats, cars and houses at the expense of the business.

Make sure you have good people all around you at management and operational levels. This allows you to grow without diluting the quality of your management and also lets your recruiters stay recruiters for longer.

Career Lessons Learned

If I had the time over I would have built and invested in the appropriate management team much more quickly during the growth phase.

With a greater number of strong managers Candle would have been able to develop the business more rapidly by opening more offices and diversifying into other non-IT lines of recruitment sooner.

I learned that going public requires a huge amount of internal resources based on a strong management and financial team. This demand continues when the new listed company has to fulfill more external reporting obligations and without good management there would be a danger of temporarily losing focus.

Recruitment in 2005

In the future I am convinced there will be continued rationalisation within the industry. Client and agency relationships will become seamless.

Master vendor, managed vendor, single vendor and on-site recruitment models are likely to become more common over the next few years as clients put more responsibility on agencies to perform the recruitment process.

Globally the Internet will continue to be a great tool in the areas of job advertising and streamlining relationships with candidates and clients.

Pressure on margins has been high in the past and clients will continue to look for better service and a capability to deliver rather than lower margins.

Geoff Morgan

As Chairman of both Morgan & Banks and TMP Australia, the world's largest human resources recruitment consultancy, Geoff Morgan oversees businesses with $1 billion in turnover and over 2,000 staff.

Geoff joined forces with Andrew Banks after meeting him at an industry function in late 1984. They opened Morgan & Banks in early 1985 with just four people including Geoff's mother, Madge, and Ian Burns. Today the Morgan & Banks Group employs over 1830 staff and has turnover of $562 million.

Geoff Morgan

The Morgan & Banks philosophy has remained consistent: to be the best not the biggest. With its innovative corporate outlook Geoff sees the company as having a definite 'do it first' attitude rather than just talking about it.

Originally Geoff's ambition was to work on the land. He started as a wool classer in the early 70s then worked in the wool industry in Australia and New Zealand while studying wool technology.

He was on a tour of Europe in 1975 when he landed his first recruiting job with Josephine Salmon. Geoff returned to Australia in 1976 and joined Executive Recruiters. He left his position of Director for Executive Recruitment in 1985 having specialised in the sales and marketing sector.

Off-line his passions are action-packed. He loves to race cars and has been Australian Porsche Cup Champion four times. In 2000 he is racing a Dodge Viper in the GT Production Nation's Cup.

Geoff and Andrew Banks share a passion for putting something back into the community. Together they developed Youth Jobs Day which has been a resounding success for the past five years, helping to reduce youth unemployment in Australia.

Geoff enjoys spending time with his three daughters and snow skiing in Australia, New Zealand and the US, heli-skiing in Canada, riding horses, breeding stud cattle, reading and savouring red wine and Italian food.

He has also been involved in a variety of other community work including the World Scout Foundation, Fundraising for Westpac Rescue Helicopter and school foundations.

Coming to work keeps Geoff stimulated. He enjoys the motivation he receives from the people and technology at Morgan & Banks. Coupled with his passion for learning and his desire to succeed, he likes nothing more than to meet new people and fuel his knowledge.

Like Andrew Banks he has a history of early entrepreneurship, maternal mentorship and a strong sense of competition. Indeed before the two had even met they were competing with each other with different restaurants in Surry Hills, NSW.

Geoff's mother taught him about integrity and instilled in him a strong sense of values, helping him to see that selling can be an honourable and exciting profession.

Enjoyment Factors

The people are the best thing. You can meet someone at an interview who might become a client or a friend for life.

I passionately believe that I can personally make a positive difference to other people's lives, making me feel I am doing something meaningful. I also realise that when I make a mistake I may hurt people. This only highlights the importance of the work I do.

When I first started nobody would talk to me because I was a recruitment consultant and they didn't believe in the profession. Now everyone wants to talk to recruiters because people's careers are so important to them and the right recruiter can make all the difference.

Inspirational People

My mother Madge Morgan inspired me - she was one of the leading salespeople in Tupperware Australia as well as succeeding in other areas such as fundraising for charities, hospitals and community groups. She is successful because people believe and trust in her. Hopefully, these are qualities that I also possess.

I am inspired by successful people who can bridge the gap between the work environment and their personal lives to create a successful balance. I am also inspired by people who can motivate and lead others by developing in them a desire to always do their very best.

Of course Andrew Banks has inspired me as my business partner due to his determination and passion to succeed.

No 1 Recruitment Success Secret

Care about your candidates. I have always said if you believe in your heart that the people you meet are important, they will feel it, whether or not you are able to place them in a new role. They will remember meeting you as a positive experience and will become a marketing tool in their own right for you. My favourite value in this industry is passion for what you do.

No 1 Manager's Success Secret

Set your philosophy and culture, then follow it. A good manager or leader will always seek out and attract the best people. This is the key to great management and leadership.

Attributes of Top Recruiters

- Caring about and growing your staff then sharing your success with them
- Excellent time management
- A desire to work with people
- An ability to handle both disappointment and success
- Resilience – being able to pick yourself up emotionally
- Being well-organised
- Doing what you say you are going to do
- Constantly following up
- Being honest
- Flexible and innovative thinking.

Advice to Recruiters Wanting To Be The Best

To recruiters who want to lead the pack I would say choose a market and specialise in it. Immerse yourself in the industry and get to know all the key people.

Be noticed. Speak at functions and write articles. Work on being known for placing the top candidates in your chosen industry and for giving excellent career advice, free of charge.

Advice to Owners & Managers Growing A Business

Share the equity in your business so that you will not lose your top people and you can delegate responsibility as your business grows.

Remember you are running a business not a consultancy therefore run a proper business - review your financials regularly, bring in outside advisors, don't try to do everything yourself such as payroll, technology, Internet and IT. Learn to partner and share.

Career Lessons Learned

I would have made most of my decisions 6-12 months sooner and would have gone global sooner. I would like to have been braver and faster and not as conservative. In some early initiatives, such as the Internet, I should have backed my judgement sooner. Basically I would do Morgan & Banks all over again.

Recruitment in 2005

The global industry is going to grow substantially in the coming five years. There will be major players and specialist boutique recruiters on a local and regional basis. There will be fewer players in the market.

First Interview

The industry needs to impose stricter standards and barriers to entry. We must create regional and global portals through partnering and encourage more industry co-operation for better outcomes for the candidates and corporate market.

Our biggest competitors in the industry are yet to enter the market. They will be global corporate entities, community groups such as trade unions and affinity groups who form their own trading cartels, which will include the careers market sector.

I believe our industry is one of the most exciting and least discovered. Its potential for growth is unlimited. The day the true worth of 'human capital' is really established will be the day the industry comes of age and realises its full value.

Bunty Paramor

Bunty Paramor's career in recruitment has spanned more than 30 years beginning in October 1968 with Key Personnel in Perth. In 1982 she took up a consultant position with PA Consulting Group in WA, became Manager of the national staff recruitment business in 1987 and went on to manage the combined executive and staff recruitment businesses in 1989.

In January 1995 she established Paramor – The Recruiters and grew the business until entering a partnership in March 1999 with Recruitment Solutions which had seen the need for a strong Western Australian presence.

Bunty Paramor

The company now has three divisions in Perth, business support, accounting and finance, sales and marketing, and recruits permanent and temporary staff at all levels. Bunty is also a member of Rotary International and enjoys the opportunity of getting involved in serving the community, both in Perth and overseas.

Her weekends generally involve her two grandchildren. She and her husband have a wide range of relaxation interests including film and theatre, gardening, dining out, walking the dog, boating, fishing and the occasional weekend away.

From the start Bunty knew she wanted a career, not just a job, and was determined to be good at whatever that turned out to be. When she fell into recruitment, by accident rather than design, she took to it straight away.

Bunty attributes her success partly to a stringent educational environment that taught her about teamwork and avoiding trouble as well as identifying and developing leadership potential.

The majority of her school years were spent in a disciplined boarding school where work, responsibility, duty and respect were all basic principles of existing and surviving the system.

This, combined with her parents' commitment and attitude toward humankind, gave her a very sound basis from the start. She says she is constantly grateful for that training, everyday, even though it would probably be considered old fashioned in today's society.

Beyond that money is a motivator for Bunty who has always wanted to be able to afford a good lifestyle and all the wonderful things and experiences the world has to offer.

Enjoyment Factors

I find so many aspects of the industry fascinating and very rewarding.

Firstly, the privileged position we are in, in terms of being trusted by both candidate and client with private, often personal, confidential information. Whether it is a candidate's hopes and dreams, successes and failures or a client's concerns about business and financial matters, we are considered trustworthy recipients of sensitive information.

Secondly, the thrill of being involved in helping someone get a job they are excited and thrilled about – perhaps one they have been wanting for ages. I know what an impact the right job in the right environment can have on a person's life when they work at full potential.

First Interview

I really enjoy assisting an organisation to identify and attract good staff who will then, in turn, help the company to be successful. This is all very powerful and satisfying for me to be involved with.

I love the variety of tasks and different locations in which our clients operate.

Recently I was in a stockbroker's boardroom, the bottling area of a vineyard and a hospital – all in one day. Great variety and interest, all important businesses, all requiring a level of understanding and knowledge from the consultant – this can be really challenging!

Another aspect I enjoy is seeing young people entering the industry and learning to become good recruiters. Seeing them succeed in a tough industry is very satisfying. I love seeing them win, developing that wonderful self-confidence that comes with winning and spurs them on to greater heights to be considered by their peers and others as true professionals.

So many consultants began their careers as juniors with me and have gone on to expand their careers. I get great satisfaction from being part of their growth and success.

Inspirational People

I read biographies and autobiographies because I enjoy learning about how successful people think, how they are motivated and how they have developed their business.

Whether it be someone as unique as Ghandi or Mother Teresa or Weary Dunlop, or a modern business tycoon like Richard Branson or Bill Gates, I learn from them.

Politicians too have a lot to offer in terms of strategic thinking and clever manipulation so I have read about Margaret Thatcher, Paul Keating, Golda Meier and John F. Kennedy among others.

The focus and determination of top athletes and performers inspire me. For example the incredible persistence with which Paralympic sprinter Louise Sauvage has overcome her physical disability to prove her worth. I always feel pretty insignificant when I see that level of human endurance and commitment.

For those of us who are fortunate enough to be born with some level of talent and a healthy body, it is our inherent duty to make every effort to use it all in a proper and directed manner.

No 1 Recruitment Success Secret

Listen to what your client wants, ask your candidate what they want – never presume. Don't tell – listen and ask. Be honest with both parties; treat everyone with respect and care.

Don't over-promise and under-deliver. Don't cut corners for a quick fee as it never works.

No 1 Manager's Success Secret

I try to stick to the philosophy of working on your business, not in it. It can be difficult sometimes but now we've got the critical mass situation this is working for me.

Be selective about the business you chase, don't price cut and seriously value your own worth.

Attributes of Top Recruiters

So many things – it depends on the exact nature of the role and the area of business.

Generally, I look for people who are bright, well educated, ambitious and motivated who are able to form good relationships with people.

They should have energy and drive, a level of street smartness, the ability to think things through logically and quickly. They need to be innovative. They must have fast recall and the ability to persuade and influence with a strong customer service focus.

Advice to Recruiters Wanting To Be The Best

As well as these personal attributes a good recruiter needs to have and demonstrate a genuine interest in the business. Work hard to be well informed and develop long-lasting relationships. Don't give up on difficult assignments.

The best recruiter wants to win and is competitive.

Advice to Owners & Managers Growing A Business

Care about your staff and train them well. Set high standards and let it be known that you expect a lot in terms of professionalism, principles and ethical behaviour.

Lead by example. Don't ask anyone to do anything you wouldn't do.

Career Lessons Learned

I would have started my own business much earlier. That's about it!

Recruitment in 2005

Obviously the technical/information era has already changed our business and will continue to do so.

Employers will still be looking for the chemistry to fit their organisational preferences – no data-based automatic CV retrieval recruitment process will replace that.

I still believe that nothing beats people meeting one another and talking, discussing with one another. When all is said and done we are the most complex animals on earth. We are still discovering how our brains work and what out personalities are about – we still have the need to see, touch, hear, even smell one another before we are comfortable. Basic animal stuff – but evolution and the new millennium hasn't changed that!

I have loved every minute of my 30+ years in the recruitment business – every day a new learning experience, everyday a new adventure. Beat that for an interesting career!

V. John Plummer

John Plummer was Managing Director of Centacom Staff Group for thirty years from 1960, during which time he built the company to fifty locations around Australia with offices in London and New Zealand. Centacom was the largest provider of permanent and temporary office staff placement services in Australia. It was sold to Swiss company Adecco in 1988 and managed by John for a further five years.

Since his formal retirement in June 1993 John has been active in the industry as Chairman of Chandler & MacLeod Consultants. He became Managing Director of Riddells Staffing in Melbourne in July 1999.

V. John Plummer

He has been President of the RCSA at state, national, and international levels and published a book in 2000 entitled, 'Staffing Consultants, A Management Guide'.

He is an active sportsman. As a middle-distance runner he represented Australia at the 1950 Auckland Empire Games and in 1956 was ranked 20th in the world in the 5,000 metres distance run. He now competes internationally in the over 70s age group in events up to 10,000 metres. He also enjoys fun runs and participates in the Sydney City to Surf event.

With this track record it is hardly surprising that John says he likes to be a winner. He got a taste for it at an early age striving to be the best at athletics, swimming, tennis and debating. He was elected School Captain but chose to assume the Vice Captaincy because his father was headmaster.

John is motivated by the challenge of competition. A good example of this is his response to the establishment of London-based Brook St. in Sydney. John was driven to constantly match their expansion and successfully preempted their interstate and suburban strategy with the growth of the Centacom business.

He observes that if he were motivated by money he wouldn't still be working now. Instead he believes that a high quality of education is very important for success in business and likes to train others to achieve mutual success. He gains a lot of job satisfaction being successful through the efforts of others, perhaps partly because he had two teachers as parents.

Enjoyment Factors

I originally trained as a chartered accountant but I prefer people rather than figures. This is why I pursued leadership roles in work, sport and associations – I have a natural desire to be a leader and a strong interest in people.

It is the nature of the recruitment industry that I really enjoy – it is very profitable with low capital investment and a high return on working capital if it is done well.

I also savour the challenge of finding the right person for the job. For 25 years I have displayed on my desk, this motto, 'The best man for the job is a woman'. I get a lot of enjoyment from finding vibrant, successful women who want to apply their personalities and ambition to achieve in recruitment.

Inspirational People

Inspiration tended not to come from others in the Australian market because we were always leading the way. I have been most inspired through my reading by authors such as Earl Nightingale, Steven Covey and Norman Vincent Peale. Dale Carnegie's book, 'How to Win Friends and Influence People' also deserves a mention.

No 1 Recruitment Success Secret

Recruiter success comes down to having a positive attitude leading to perseverance and a refusal to accept knock-backs. To be able to sustain positive action to continually search for the right person for the client, the recruiter must believe in action rather than thinking or talking about it. A high energy level is important, even without very long hours.

No 1 Manager's Success Secret

To be successful a manager or business owner you must choose the best people. Only employ the best and never accept mediocrity. By this I don't mean seek superior people but rather to see the potential in people you employ. Don't overlook personality: clients and applicants will respond best to someone who is outgoing, warm and pleasantly assertive.

Attributes of Top Recruiters

The best recruiters have these characteristics in common:
• They are pleasantly assertive as opposed to aggressive. Smiling, warm-hearted people do best.
• They are commercially qualified, they know the market they are recruiting in.
• They must have commitment, dedication, perseverance and ability to accept rejection.
• They have a desire for recognition, advancement and a high income.

Sales ability is not essential although it is a distinct advantage, but it is not good to be restricted to recruiters who are too pushy. The best recruiter is one who understands sales techniques (you can teach them) yet gives their clients the impression they are not too sales oriented. Success will come from matching the right people to a job. Even if the recruiter doesn't have sales ability, good presentation and recruitment skills will cause the sale to happen anyway.

Recruiters also need to have a willingness to learn, have confidence, are liked and are trusted.

Creative thinking helps to cross sell candidates among clients. Core skills in one profession are often transferable to other industries although it does require some selling skills to get people to switch professions.

V. John Plummer

Advice to Recruiters Wanting To Be The Best

Observe those who are the best and copy their style.

Do further training to learn more and make sure time management is a priority so that quality time with the right people yields consistent performance. Helping new recruits is important to bring experienced people back to basics and tighten up their skills.

I encourage self-improvement – pay attention to your dress, voice, learning and skills training and read motivational books with success stories.

Advice to Owners & Managers Growing A Business

My advice to owners and business managers would be to identify and commit to your mission, goals and long term plans. Don't grow for growth's sake but keep to business sectors that are profitable and make best use of your expertise. Fast growth should happen through mergers and acquisitions and through developing and promoting your best people.

Follow Key Performance Indicators to show you are on track keeping an eye on profit, cashflow, placement ratios, advertising response, applicant utilisation and industry performance indicators. Survey your own market to appreciate its size, competition sources and identify problems and opportunities early in the process.

Career Lessons Learned

Importantly Centacom had a very successful 30 years of growth with a profitable sale to Adecco in December 1988. However with the benefit of hindsight I would have done some things differently.

I would have delegated the management and training function sooner. I took a while to have the courage to place people in senior positions but when I put managers in place, locally and interstate, the business really expanded.

I would have allowed Centacom more time to diversify and grow into other markets such as medical, industrial and executive. I see now that it would have been better to have a one-stop shop rather than a high volume office support niche. If growth is the aim then diversification of services is needed.

I chose not to employ sales staff even though some of the bigger agencies had success using sales people to bring in new business. This would have grown my business faster but possibly at the expense of the high levels of client and candidate service which come from one-on-one relationships.

In hindsight I would not buy my own premises again. I had capital tied up in the ownership of 20 sites and I only made normal real estate returns with limited capital gains. I now believe long-term leasing can still protect the company's goodwill and provide stability, flexibility and more working capital.

I would have been tighter on debtor days outstanding, reducing them from 40 to 28 days.

I could have made the company leaner and meaner to make more working capital available for expansion or investment in other revenue generating activities such as the share market or overseas partnerships

Recruitment in 2005

The industry is still growing. In the future I estimate that 25 per cent of the workforce will be part-time, temporary or on contract. There will be growth in part-time and temporary as these areas increase in acceptance. Permanent employment will grow as the image of recruitment firms steadily improves and specialists are shown to really help clients.

Executive headhunting will grow as the need for quality people continues to dominate. I predict 10 per cent growth per annum in volume.

The industry needs to increase its support and loyalty to the RCSA because its programs are beneficial to everyone. The industry really must get stronger on regulation and the policing of ethics, particularly where pirating of staff and temps is concerned.

I would like to see education being more available and encouraged. A more active political stance through lobbying is needed to improve the legislation. Importantly relationships with unions need attention to ensure they continue to develop positively.

Raymond Roe

Ray Roe became Chief Executive Officer of Adecco Group, Asia Pacific, in 1998. The organisation has a turnover in excess of 2 billion and a regional headcount of 2000. Australia accounts for 35 per cent of the Group's revenues with 500 employees.

He has had a varied career including 26 years in the US Army. Ray retired in 1993 with the rank of Brigadier General, having commanded units around the world.

Ray's last military appointment was with the Community and Family Support Centre where he was responsible for facilities such as hotels, childcare and personnel amenities on bases around the globe. He managed the development of a scheme to purchase a hotel in Disney World for use by military and their families.

In September 1993 Ray effected a significant career change and became branch manager of a four-person office in Atlanta for the well-known outplacement company, Lee Hecht Harrison. Soon after he took on the role of Regional Head of Southern US and in 1996 became Chief Operating Officer of the company.

Travel, running and movies figure largely in the way he spends his hard-earned spare time. However these may have to take second place in his affections now that he has become a proud grandfather.

Like all successful recruiters Ray enjoys facing challenges. In his life he has always taken hold of chances to be a player on a bigger stage, such as running in the Boston Marathon and moving his career to Australia to take on a larger role.

He appreciates success, regardless how it is measured, and is greatly motivated by building on strengths and encouraging teamwork to help people be more successful than they thought possible.

Enjoyment Factors

I like people. One of the things I love about this industry is that it attracts people who know how to care and nurture others. According to some this is why women have been so successful in our company and our industry.

I enjoy having the opportunity to build a team that can deliver a better service. That's all about building a culture of service. Service excellence enables any size company to outperform a larger company – a service culture is the key to added value.

Inspirational People

The people who have inspired me have all helped me to understand that it's important to not give up, to never quit.

My first job was in the army as a field artillery Lieutenant. Sergeant First Class White, who was responsible for the artillery pieces in the battery, supposedly reported to me. The Sergeant was a big man, as old as my father. He knew everything about his job – people and the guns. He said if I listened and did what he told me to do he would make me the best officer in the army.

At Lee Hecht Harrison I was responsible for buying a business with a partner who was an IT specialist building a program for outplacement. I was impressed with her clarity for vision and her skill at articulating how technology could help the business succeed rather than how fancy it could be.

Lastly Peter Snell, middle distance runner, was a huge inspiration. He was a legend for hard training and practice. Most of my achievements are linked to running. It changed my life and helped me get into West Point and earn respect as an officer because I was so physically fit.

No 1 Recruitment Success Secret

Focus. A recruiter is deluged with lots of information at one time but must be able to prioritise. That means focusing on one job at a time while still taking in everything else that is happening.

Keep in touch with the candidate and client to make sure things happen. Always know what the next step is to make the placement

No 1 Manager's Success Secret

A manager's success is all about people – leading, managing, demonstrating and motivating your staff. People need to see you are part of the team. You must also be looking to the horizon to where the company is heading.

Attributes of Top Recruiters

- Have discipline – go through all the steps, gather all the available information, pay attention to detail
- Be very organised during the process
- Be focused on objectives – think outside the nine dots. Ask, 'how does the candidate's experience match the requirements?' Sometimes the answers are not the obvious ones.

Advice to Recruiters Wanting To Be The Best

To be the best you have to be part of a team and recognise the contribution of others. You cannot do anything alone – as in anything in life.

That means three things:
- Stay humble – remember you are in service to the industry
- Always listen to others
- Keep an eye on the task at hand i.e. filling the job while being alert for good candidates for assignments you don't have.

Advice to Owners & Managers Growing A Business

Owners and managers need to know what to look for in several ways. For example if a person on your staff doesn't fit into the company and its values, make a decision early to terminate the relationship. In the same way be wary of the 'gun' recruiter because they often come to you from someone else for a reason – they will come with some baggage and sometimes hard-to-manage egos.

When recruiting your own people look for the right attitude not just previously demonstrated performance or experience. If they have the attitude you can train them to recruit.

Finally go after the small deals; lots of small deals will grow a business. Don't waste time chasing too many rabbits because you won't catch one.

Career Lessons Learned

Over my career I have learned a couple of important lessons. The priority must be to build a strong management team even though it takes time and might seem unnecessary. This will definitely pay off later.

Secondly, you've got to make sure the back of house works – the systems, invoicing, administration. If these are not in order it will show, no matter how well things appear to be going.

Recruitment in 2005

Despite short-term ups and downs in the economy, the long-term dynamic is that the industry is in an extraordinary growth phase and is likely to be healthier in 2005 than it is now. I predict 10 to 15 per cent growth in sales over each of the next five years.

There are several reasons for this:
• Large companies are recognising that to be competitive in a world market, they must be competitive in their well-defined core business. Companies will recognise recruiting is not among their core competencies.
• Smaller companies (where the biggest growth will be) will also realise that it is less expensive and more efficient for them to avoid spending precious time on the very detailed and time consuming recruitment process.
• There will continue to be fast job growth in the temp/casual market, encompassing people who previously were not part of the labour force.

Within the industry smaller players will be squeezed out as margins get smaller. The industry needs to develop principals to assure our clients and candidates of our integrity and honesty. We must be seen as an industry with its act together. As well there is a need to guarantee our work with a minimum time period for permanent and temp staff.

An essential area for scrutiny is confidentiality. We have to display and demonstrate an absolute, flawless level of confidentiality for candidates and clients. With the use of Web sites and email, the industry needs to establish standards, particularly in terms of confidentiality of candidate information. A job board will not solve the recruitment problem. We need to ask, 'Is the job board an advertising place or a vehicle to use the data for other purpose?'

Julia Ross

Julia Ross is Managing Director of Julia Ross Recruitment Limited – a 100 per cent Australian-owned international recruitment group scheduled for listing on the Australian Stock Exchange in 2000.

Julia established the company as Julia Ross Personnel in 1988 with a staff of one. Twelve years and many awards later she runs a multi-million dollar business that employs almost 200. The company supports eleven offices throughout Australia, seven specialist divisions, and a fully Australian-owned international operation based in London.

Julia Ross

Julia is very much a hands-on Managing Director, regularly visiting all her operations in both Australia and London and maintaining a strong service presence with key client accounts.

When she is not at the helm of her growing business, Julia particularly enjoys spending time with her young son, as well as exercising, catching up with friends and relaxing at her country property in Scone, NSW.

Julia is proud of her achievements in creating, building and successfully managing an international company. Throughout this process she has applied her strengths in understanding people and markets to develop a valuable brand, securing some of Australia's largest recruitment contracts based on a reputation for superior service standards.

She has nurtured a positive and rewarding career environment for her team members, many of whom have stayed with her throughout years of considerable growth and change. The company actively supports an internal promotional philosophy that encourages growth and career development for everyone in the business.

Julia grew up in a large family dominated by older brothers. Her mother, a strong personality and great promoter of equality between the sexes, had a weighty influence on the beliefs and expectations Julia formed growing up.

Coupled with this influence was the impact of being surrounded by males who developed career paths and opportunities unfettered by the significant gender protocols that still pervaded working life in the 1970s.

Julia embarked on her career in the male-dominated construction industry where her determination and genuine interest in people, together with the strong support of two encouraging mentors, motivated her to overcome a range of gender-based prejudices. Her success in that sector led to her being selected as a finalist in the Veuve Cliquot Business Woman of the Year Awards at 21 years of age.

Her people-orientated approach was a strong motivator for Julia when moving into a senior role with international recruiter Alfred Marks, and remains a key component of the management of her business today.

Julia is also driven to provide her son with the type of secure, balanced, driven and secure home environment she values so highly.

In talking with Julia it is clear that the word 'failure' is just not in her vocabulary. She sets high expectations for herself – and often for those around her

– and does not rest until the results she achieves meet or exceed her expectations. Her energy and sense of purpose have a strong impact on all who come into contact with her.

Enjoyment Factors

I have always had so much fun with my business. I find it extremely dynamic and I never forget to have a laugh as well.

My business involves making lots of decisions, problem solving, thinking on my feet and dealing with ever-changing and unpredictable market conditions. I love the challenge of never knowing what is going to confront me each day.

Perhaps that's a reason why women do very well in this industry – they are good at having to juggle lots of priorities at once, meet the sometimes conflicting needs of different people and still keep their heads above water! I've never felt a barrier to success in this industry.

Inspirational People

Throughout my career mentors have been really important in inspiring me.

In the construction industry I really appreciated my mentors because they treated me with equality and recognised my strengths, giving me the chance to use my initiative and try new things.

Their confidence in me as they constantly challenged me to succeed allowed me to rise quickly to a high level. One mentor put me on a number of senior management courses when I was quite young, providing a good foundation for managing my own business. It helped me to believe I could do anything.

A person who stands out is Laurence Rosen, National Operations Director at Alfred Marks, who had responsibility for 120 branches. He was the most talented recruitment manager I have ever seen and taught me lots about marketing. Laurence was a showman and very courageous with his innovative marketing ideas.

No 1 Recruitment Success Secret

Although I was always a manager, not a recruiter, I believe the most important success secret is being able to manage your time well. A successful recruiter will be selfish with their time and get things to completion fast, given they are good at communicating and accessing needs.

No 1 Manager's Success Secret

A manager today must be more than just that – they must truly be a leader. This involves having good judgement, an ability to make decisions quickly and solve problems. They must be able to relate to their people well enough to know how to deliver their decisions positively and motivate people within the requirements of the business.

Attributes of Top Recruiters

Recruiters need a broad perspective on life, with many experiences to draw on giving them empathy to understand other people's perspectives. They also need to develop good communication skills, apply attention to detail and work with a sense of urgency.

It is important for them to be highly driven; they must be high achievers and enjoy constant challenge. Top achievers need a high sense of reward so that they are continually learning and growing.

They must have the ability to build high-level relationships. I often find new staff working in other service industries and I choose them because they have a track record of good service and client empathy.

Advice to Recruiters Wanting To Be The Best

First and foremost, to succeed you have to be tenacious – keep going until the job is done and work on being good at completion. Look at new ways of succeeding every day and strive for constant improvement.

It's important to have a genuine interest in the business of the clients you're working with. This will help you build a strong commercial awareness and it will be easier to make a priority of really understanding the client's business in its entirety.

The other important side of the equation of course is a great ability to relate to candidates and to win their confidence. They'll know if you don't really care about their needs, and they won't trust you when you put them into a job. You have to have a genuine interest.

Advice to Owners & Managers Growing A Business

It is my belief that a recruiting business can't grow if the manager is also recruiting so it's essential to institute policies and procedures early on for passing on to new staff. Many companies have problems if this is done too late – service levels and quality will drop.

When that is in place make sure you know your business in every small detail and then go out and sell, sell, sell. Develop a growth plan strategy in advance and place emphasis on thorough financial planning.

Keep yourself well-informed about market changes such as technology and legislation and lastly, have the courage to stand by your own principles and values.

Career Lessons Learned

With hindsight I would have aimed to grow more quickly but you can't get somewhere unless you know where you're going. On that note, I would have enjoyed having international presence in Europe and America.

I realise I should have replaced myself earlier to give the company the opportunity to expand into other countries and markets more quickly.

This is to say that if I had replaced myself earlier in the very operational end of the business, I would have had more time to work on my business strategically, leading our expansion sooner.

Recruitment in 2005

Unlike some I don't believe technology will fully replace recruitment although there will be inevitable rationalisation and a reduction in the number of smaller players. There will need to be a focus on streamlining delivery to clients.

The industry as a whole needs to become more organised, developing a common voice and lobbying the government to ensure protection in terms of legislative changes, regulation and licensing. This will improve ethics and inspire a more sophisticated industry as exists in some other countries.

Greg Savage

Greg Savage is a leading authority on consultant performance and management. He has been dedicated in experimenting, learning and sharing his findings on this most critical aspect of recruitment company performance.

In 1987 Greg co-founded Recruitment Solutions. By 1998, he and his colleagues had built sales of Recruitment Solutions to $50 million and had a staff of 150 working out of eight offices in five states. Greg played an integral role in the successful public listing of the company in July 1998.

Greg Savage

In 2000 Greg left Recruitment Solutions to spend time with his family, conduct hugely successful industry seminars and take a long break in Italy and France.

Born in Cape Town, South Africa, Greg completed his Bachelor of Social Science at the University of Cape Town before moving to Adelaide to study a Diploma of Applied Psychology at Flinders University.

His first three years in recruitment were at John P Young and Associates in Adelaide, one of the founders of advertised selection in Australia. In 1982 Greg moved to London for a two-year stint as a Manager of six permanent consultants at Accountancy Personnel, (now Hays Group) in London. He then transferred to the Sydney office, managing 25 consultants and was appointed to the Board of this international company at the age of 28.

Greg is very clear about what has driven and motivated him to succeed in his recruitment career. He has a passion for the business, and a belief in the real value for money it provides when operating at its best for both clients and candidates. He is inspired by the symmetry of success in recruitment – a perfect triangle of win, win, win for the client, the candidate and the recruiter!

He was driven by the negative view of the industry in the late 80s and was challenged to re-educate people, set a higher standard and deliver above expectations. He found it intensely rewarding when previously skeptical clients start to view recruiters as solution providers rather than 'body shops'.

Greg's personality responds well to the competitive nature of the industry which he considers to be 'one big arm wrestle'.

He is fascinated and motivated by the intrinsically measurable nature of the recruitment business. He has found that there is nowhere to hide in recruitment. A recruiter either wins the sale, closes the deal, writes the fees and makes the profit – or they don't! It's the sort of business where there are no prizes for coming second. Greg has observed that most people who have done well in recruitment respond well to these conditions.

Enjoyment Factors

I really enjoy recruitment, as it is an industry where you can make things happen. With most jobs it is difficult to measure your impact. In recruitment you can really affect outcomes with a quick return on your efforts.

For example after just a few days of mentoring and coaching it is possible to quickly turn around a non-performing office or individual. People will respond very quickly to appropriate input and, in our business, this can flow on to improved results fast. Its tremendously rewarding to be involved in turnarounds of this kind. Managing or leading recruiting teams can be intensely rewarding because you can see the impact of your leadership (positively or negatively) almost straight away.

I find the competitive nature of recruitment appealing, because you always know whether you are winning or losing – daily, weekly or monthly.

As recruitment is a relatively young industry, the rules are still being defined and change is exciting and constant. There are plenty of opportunities to be innovative, to develop different products and services and to deliver better, more consistent service. It is exhilarating to work in an industry where it has not all been done before.

Finally the recruitment industry provides tremendous satisfaction from leveraging off the efforts of others, whether they are temps or recruitment consultants – all of whom also benefit from your recruitment efforts.

Inspirational People

There are many people I have admired and learned from in the recruitment industry, and there are a few who really stand out. The person who has inspired me the most is Graham Whelan, fellow Director when I was at Recruitment Solutions.

Put simply, I really admired Graham's:
• Incredible energy
• Positive attitude
• Constant looking for the good in people
• Intense listening skills even after 20 years in the industry
• Lack of jaded cynicism
• High levels of customer service
• Natural, built-in, non-negotiable ethics and values.

Throughout 13 years of building Recruitment Solutions, Graham was very supportive when we had our inevitable setbacks. He continued to have faith in me and the business – even in tough situations. He really is a reservoir of positive thinking.

Some of the smaller recruiters, who keep going without the financial and human resources of big companies, also inspire me. There are many such people running great businesses through out Australia. People like Kaye

Straine at Futures in Sydney for example. I admire the tenacity of these business people and the quality of the work they produce, sometimes with limited resources.

Furthermore, I found the history of Morgan & Banks inspirational. Although I may not embrace their ethos or some of their competitive tactics, Morgan & Banks have showed us that we can take our industry more seriously. They are constantly re-creating themselves, ahead of the game and have made hundreds of people wealthy while delivering results to their shareholders. They have shown the path for many other recruiters to grow and list.

I have absorbed ideas and strengths from hundreds of people working at the recruitment coalface. I recognise and applaud the perseverance and strength of character many of these people possess.

No 1 Recruitment Success Secret

While I was a good recruiter and not a great recruiter, I knew to sweat the small stuff and do the numbers. I also learned early that if you want to avoid frustration and serious hits to your self-esteem it is important to view yourself as an equal to both clients and candidates, then build strong relationships and take control of the recruitment process. Make sure you run your job. Don't let the job run you.

All great consultants adhere to what I call the 'Recruiters Success Formula', that is, Success = Activity x Quality (of that activity) x Target Market (with the right people).

I passionately believe consultants can maximise productivity without working overly long hours and burning out.

No1 Manager's Success Secret

Hire people around you that are better than you at what you are currently doing. Then go out and do different and new things to grow your business. Hire attitude and not just experience or qualifications.

Apply the Activity x Quality x Target Market formula which will flow to the bottom line and maximise business performance.

Attributes Of Top Recruiters

I separate the attributes of top recruiters into three categories – Intrinsic Attributes (your personality profile – what you are), Learned Skills (what you know) and Attitudes (how you think and behave).

Intrinsic Attributes
- Competitive by nature
- Passionate about recruiting
- Perseverance and tenacity
- Work ethic
- Initiative
- Integrity.

Learned skills
- Product knowledge
- Planning and prioritising skills
- People and market assessment
- Client and candidate control skills
- Listening skills
- Negotiation skills
- Understanding that consistent quantity of quality activity leads to results.

Attitudes
- Being a 'can do' person
- Opportunistic
- Team worker
- Having a value-add attitude
- Continuous learning attitude
- Sales belief.

Advice to Recruiters Wanting To Be The Best

Avoid complacency, as you will get results early on, but not all the time. Add to your 'skills briefcase' so that you are always employable, especially with the onset of Internet recruitment.

Review your 'skills balance sheet' every six months to ensure you keep adding techniques the market demands. Develop skills that provide solutions for clients and candidates.

In summary, if you want to be the best there are three Rs – Resume (add to your skills,) Reputation (your activities adding to your reputation) and your Rolodex (add to and nurture your contacts). Keep reviewing the 3 Rs constantly.

Advice To Owners & Managers Growing A Business

Put 70 per cent of your time into hiring, coaching and developing your people. At all costs, do not accept mediocrity in your business. Give people the opportunity to be successful with support and coaching, but be prepared to cut your losses if consultants consistently under-perform.

I estimate it costs $75,000 – $100,000 to keep a recruiter at their desk and the opportunity cost of poor performers can be huge. When spread over a number of people it can be crippling to your business.

Again, always manage your business on Activity x Quality x Target Market. Don't manage on emotion or gut feeling. You can't manage what you can't measure, therefore measure the key activities that lead to success.

Career Lessons Learned

There are many lessons I have learned and several things I would have, in hindsight, done differently.

I would have concentrated more on hiring people who had intrinsic attributes suitable for becoming good recruiters and managers, instead of a solely a track record in other industries.

I wouldn't have made the mistake of assuming all great recruiters can manage people, and would have created more careers in recruitment rather than in management. There are many incentives and challenges for recruiters outside of management.

I should have given greater working flexibility for consulting and support staff sooner, by offering staggered hours, part-time consulting, working from home and job-sharing.

We should have diversified the business earlier by broadening the service offer to clients with related products and services. It may have been smart to put more effort into developing a brand, because the power of a brand's credibility is more important than I initially recognised. When you sell or list, the brand is very important for business value, recognition and credibility.

We also should have put more effort into staff retention and communication strategies much earlier. We could have hired specialist support people, including marketing and HR staff, earlier in the company's history rather than later in the growth process. As the business grows, line managers can easily be swamped with non-core yet still important tasks which impinge on financial performance (and stress levels!)

We could have created the Team Leader role sooner so that ambitious consultants had more opportunity to develop management, leadership and mentoring skills.

Recruitment In 2005

By 2005 I believe the industry will have evolved substantially so that 70 per cent of the market is controlled by major multi-nationals and large players, with the remainder of firms in the hands of high-quality, niche, specialist recruiters.

Client expectations of service delivery will have risen significantly and consultants will fall into two categories:
1) Highly skilled solution providers.
2) Moderately paid resourcers.

Profits, expressed as EBIT to Sales, will have dropped due to Internet recruitment forcing down traditional cost structures and margins. Yet, contrary to the majority view, I do not believe that Internet recruitment will dominate or destroy the traditional recruitment model due to the strong reliance on relationships in the recruitment process.

Internet recruiting will have gone full circle, so that this sector of the industry will have also rationalised, leaving the market with a handful of major job boards. There will be a convergence of Internet and traditional recruitment so that all major recruiters will embrace the Internet as part of their business model.

Rosemary Scott

With her eyes fixed firmly on her goals, British-born Rosemary Scott grew her own successful business called Scotstaff between 1976 and 1990. As Director and then Managing Director she saw the company expand from general Secretarial/Office Support into Financial Services and Insurance. She then sold the company to Chandler Recruitment Services in time to realise her dream of retiring at the age of 40.

In 1992 Rosemary came out of retirement and formed Scott Training & Consulting, now Scott Recruitment Services. She is the first Australian trainer and recruiter of recruitment consultants with offices in Sydney, Melbourne, Brisbane and more recently London.

She has held senior positions with the IPC, including NSW Director in 1983-1990 and 1993-1997 and Australasian President from 1987-1990. She was also the NSW President of the NAPC from 1985-1988 and sat on the National Board from 1986-1990.

As well as her intimate knowledge of the workings of the industry Rosemary has a real love and enthusiasm for recruitment consulting. This is a strong motivating force along with her vision for succeeding in providing recruitment services to the recruitment industry in Australia.

Enjoyment Factors

I get a lot of satisfaction from dealing every day with clients and candidates who share a similar enthusiasm and passion for the industry. Recruitment is rare because there are no glass ceilings – women can be just as successful in this industry as men. That is very unusual in the business world.

Another unique characteristic of the recruitment industry is that people who are prepared to work hard are rewarded at a level commensurate with the amount of work they put in. It's possible to earn exceptionally large amounts of money if you are an achiever.

Inspirational People

John Plummer Snr. is a great inspiration because he has believed in and supported the many capable women in the industry. John has commanded tremendous staff loyalty by granting his managers true autonomy and rewarding them very well.

Joan May (Premier Staff later part of ADIA group, now ADECCO) has also inspired me. I followed Joan as NSW NAPC President and IPC Australasian President. She was an efficient committee member who handled many different meetings and issues. She was strong on ethics, principals and values, with total dedication to the industry, one of those people who donated lots of time that they could have been spending on their business.

I also must mention Barbara Smith, Managing Director of BAS, which was later taken over by Kelly Services. Just as John Plummer was known as the father of the industry, Barbara was the aunt of the industry. She worked in the same building as Scotstaff and was a great example of how to maintain a solid reputation while building a company.

First Interview

Finally I have to tell a quick story of my first day in the industry in 1973. I almost left then and there because I was working with a branch manager who spent the whole day talking to clients and candidates about herself non-stop! I was saved by my Regional Manager, Irene Herd, who wisely moved me to another office where I received excellent training. Irene was my mentor in the early days. She taught me all about recruitment in the early 70s and became by business partner at Scotstaff.

No 1 Recruitment Success Secret

The secrets of recruitment success are persistence and communication. Real persistence is a quality few people have and it is so important. Consultants must be prepared to work hard, take knockbacks and not take it personally.

Communication is also important as this is a people industry. Effective communication is necessary to understand your client and candidate requirements which in turn will make you a more effective recruiter.

No 1 Manager's Success Secret

Be an inspirational leader and a motivator of staff. To do this you have to lead from the front and show your staff you can do the job as well as they can.

Continually motivate your staff to excel and succeed by encouragement, consistent and generous rewards. To err on the side of generosity is better for the business than putting the money in your pocket. Furthermore, effectively communicate your feedback on your staff's performance so that they know where they stand and how they are performing.

Attributes of Top Recruiters

Consultants need to be innovative and intelligent and must have a sense of humour to be able to have a laugh and enjoy work.

As well as these personality traits, there are some characteristics that everyone in the industry should aim to develop.
- Persistence – Consultants must see the recruitment process through, to work hard and keep trying. Things just don't happen immediately. It can take six calls to gain entry to a new client. Most recruiters give up after three calls.
- Communication – The recruitment business is all about communicating successfully with clients and candidates to match their needs accurately. Communication is not just about talking; listening and questioning are the most important attributes of a good recruiter.

- Negotiation Skills – Most recruitment activity revolves around negotiation regarding salary, fees, and much more. This is an important skill for consultants to have or else to learn fast.
- Multi-tasking – It's important to juggle many things at once. Consultants need to have a quick and active mind, be flexible thinkers and recognise there are many alternative ways to making a successful placement.
- Intestinal fortitude – To put it bluntly, consultants need guts. By that I mean staying power as well as a healthy mind and body. Along with physical fitness, successful consultants must possess strong personal values and be able to balance work and play.

Advice to Recruiters Wanting To Be The Best

My advice to recruiters would be to not concentrate on the dollars, but concentrate on the service. If you do the best for your clients and candidates the dollars will follow automatically.

That means paying attention to the quality of your client list which will subsequently determine the quality and flow of your candidates.

Be prepared to work hard, be responsive to good training and put this training into effect on the job to achieve your goals.

Advice to Owners & Managers Growing A Business

For the record I want to say to business owners: Your greatest challenge in this business will not be your clients and candidates, it will be your staff.

Treat your staff as you would your clients. In the words of American small business guru, Michael Gerber, work on the business not in the business so that, you can lead, motivate and inspire others to do the work and grow your company.

Career Lessons Learned

I realise now that I could have grown Scotstaff much more if I had opened other offices and taken Michael Gerber's advice myself. Instead I recruited full-time and I believe my thinking was too small and restrictive. The business could have grown substantially larger and become more valuable if I had been more open to change and growth.

Also I think forty was too early to retire. My advice to people retiring early would be to get involved with something else, rather than sitting on the farm as I did playing with my horses and cows.

First Interview

Recruitment in 2005

The industry will continue to be highly competitive, with even more new recruitment companies. I firmly believe there needs to be some restriction in licensing to control what is a very important job – managing people's careers.

I predict that recruitment will be fast, highly computerised and Internet-driven. Players will either be large global players or specialist, boutique operations. Mid-sized companies will be squeezed as they will not be able to compete with global players on price and candidate flow. Being generalists they won't be able to withstand competition from niche firms who are focused on one specialty.

Geoff Slade

As Chairman and Chief Executive of the Geoff Slade Group, Geoff Slade continues to be at the forefront of the Personnel Industry. The Geoff Slade Group includes the Lyncroft Consulting Group which focuses on executive recruitment and training. Lyncroft has formed an alliance with Adecco. Together they are the official staffing services supporters of the Sydney 2000 Olympic Games. Other divisions of the group are Slade & Partners (executive search), GSH Personnel (office services and temporary help) and Lyncroft IT.

Geoff Slade

Geoff negotiated the sale of his company, the Slade Consulting Group, to a major British multi-national in 1988 after building it up from an initial capital base of $300 in 1968.

He is conscious of the fact that, during his 33 years in the industry, he has had the opportunity to impact the lives and careers of thousands of recruitment professionals.

In that time he has had the chance to train many who today are leaders in the industry themselves. These include Andrew Banks, Peter Tanner, Jim Bailey, David Reddin, Nan Carroll and Malcolm Jackman, to name a few.

Geoff oversaw the 1996 merger of the NAPC and IPC industry bodies. As the current and founding chairman of the RCSA, he has been instrumental in turning it into the body it is today.

It has often been said of Geoff that he personally probably knows more business people in Australia than any other person. He is also a former Chairman and active member of the Young President's Organisation.

As well as spending time with his wife and four children, Geoff has maintained an avid interest in sport, particularly AFL, cricket and golf. His Lyncroft Estate vineyard and winery at Red Hill on Mornington Peninsula has enjoyed success as a finalist for the 1998 Jimmy Watson trophy, and has won gold medals at the Royal Melbourne show.

By his own account Geoff hailed from humble beginnings, growing up in country Victoria. His parents ran a general store, which was open 7 days, and there he learned an important work ethic. Geoff worked 4-7pm every night after school and every weekend. There he developed a desire to be respected in the community for being good at what he did.

He is driven now by the challenge of business in the general sense and the fact that he loves what he does and is still passionate about it after 33 years.

Enjoyment Factors

My enjoyment in this business comes from the cut and thrust; the fact that it is a highly competitive industry. I love the people interaction and the business development side of the business.

Inspirational People

My parents provided the first inspiration in my life. I was born when my father was 60 and my mother 38. As they were quite old and in poor health in my developmental years, I was inspired to put my family first. I later realised how much they had provided for my sister and me despite them not having much money. They were completely selfless.

My second inspiration was footballer, Ron Barassi, who was my mentor when I was his understudy at the Melbourne football club in the 1963-1965. His greatest achievement was making me realise, albeit unwittingly, that I wasn't going to be as good as him and I should concentrate on business.

My wife has been a real inspiration to me. After the end of my first marriage she has helped me to be a better person and less self-centred. Lastly, I am inspired by my children, who I think are fantastic, and will hopefully help make the world a better place.

No 1 Recruitment Success Secret

The most important secret for recruitment success is to understand your customer's needs – including the needs and expectations of both the client and the candidate.

No 1 Manager's Success Secret

To succeed today as a business owner a manager needs to understand that today's candidate is tomorrow's client. The result will be to treat them with respect and responsiveness to build the relationship and protect its future.

Attributes of Top Recruiters

Apart from the relationship priorities I have already mentioned, a recruiter must bring to the job tenacity and perseverance, good communication and presentation skills. Nothing can replace an ability to build trust; successful recruitment is about honesty and being prepared to say what you think even if the client doesn't like it.

To be successful today, you need to be an all round business adviser, not just someone who can put a 'bum on a seat'. Overall you have to love what you do and be passionate about it.

Advice to Recruiters Wanting To Be The Best

My advice to recruiters who want to be on top is this:
• Work hard
• Have fun

- Love what you do
- Have integrity
- Be honest in your approach.

You have to have a balanced business focus with an eye on the short- and the long-term and you need to be a good relationship builder.

Advice to Owners & Managers Growing A Business

You can't grow a business unless you are prepared to take risks. However you shouldn't go too far out on a limb financially. You need to see that the business goes in cycles and be prepared to take tough decisions where necessary.

People are so important. Understand where you are today and where you want to go and communicate that to your staff – they have to share your vision. Pay your people well and demand a lot of them. It is essential to keep challenging your people.

You need to stay up-to-date with the latest business thinking. I think part of the reason for my success is that I have been prepared to continually invest in my own education through the Stamford Executive program 1997-1999 and the Harvard Owners and Presidents program. After the Stamford program I grew my business from $920,000 to $10 million in 3 years and, having just completed the Harvard program, my current business has grown 60 per cent in one year. There must be some correlation – much of this growth has come from big preferred suppliers, rather than lots of small transactions.

Success is closely linked to being able to find and hire the right people. Like doctors many businesses are good at helping their clients but don't look after themselves.

Career Lessons Learned

In the early days I was still learning to appreciate that the key factor in this industry is to understand your customer's needs in detail. Over time I developed an emphasis on honesty, integrity and treating people equally which is important to me today.

With the benefit of hindsight I would have worked harder to keep Andrew Banks in the business in the mid-80s. He may have made me a lot more money than I have made myself.

Recruitment in 2005

The whole scene will change enormously with ongoing consolidation due to the advent of globalisation. To play with the big boys, players will need access to capital and a heavy investment in technology. Companies will need both a bricks and mortar and on-line strategy or, as we say today, 'clicks and mortar'.

There will be no more middle ground. The guys in the middle will be swallowed up, making it necessary to be either a major player or a boutique operator. Fundamentally, there will be a lot fewer companies in the industry and survival will be more difficult.

As ever the emphasis will be on customer service. With increasing pressure from unions, legislation and the like, the industry needs a common voice. While the RCSA currently represents 900 members, all firms need to join to make it a more cohesive, viable and meaningful body. To paraphrase President John F. Kennedy, 'Ask not what your industry can do for you, ask what you can do for it.'

Peter Tanner

Peter Tanner, Principal, Tanner Menzies, brings a vast range of industry experience to his role. He embodies the philosophy of Tanner Menzies through his professionalism, reliability, sharp business focus and commitment to customer service.

Before founding Tanning Menzies Peter was General Manager of a large Australian biomedical company. He is degree-qualified in Accounting and has over 26 years' experience in business, the depth of which is reflected in his leadership of Tanner Menzies.

Peter Tanner

The company employs 150 people in offices around Australia and has an annual turnover of $20 million.

Peter has a reputation for being an ethical, straight-forward recruiter and is deeply committed to his work as Chairman of Reach Youth, a Victorian charity for young people aged 13-18 years.

A keen supporter of Geelong Football Club, Peter lives on a farm in Moorooduc, past Frankston, Victoria, where he raises alpacas.

Peter grew up in humble beginnings and learned early on that success will come if you are really driven to do something; if you put your mind to it. He has always wanted to prove to people that he could do anything he set out to do and that is still a driving force in his life.

Enjoyment Factors

The industry is exciting and every day is different. I appreciate how well the industry has grown, both professionally and in reputation. When we first started there was a sense that we somehow had to apologise for what we did, for being what we were. Today the industry is working better together – even as competitors, and I love the enthusiasm and focus of the people within our industry.

We are privileged to have what I like to call a 'helicopter view' of the Australian economy, because this industry provides us with a unique perspective on what is happening everywhere.

I also really enjoy the process of winning business. Clients today are more educated about what we do and the value we can add to their business. As a result they are willing to share their business plans with us so that we can be true consultants.

Inspirational People

There are a number of people who have inspired me to succeed and to whom I am really grateful.

- Geoff Slade taught me the value of looking after people outside the work environment. He is a tough man but treats everyone equally.
- Jim Bailey had great belief in me and encouraged me to achieve beyond the bounds of what I thought I could.
- Mark Emerson, one of my partners at Tanner Menzies, inspires me because he just wants to do it and be the best we can.

- Peter Gleeson, the third principal at Tanner Menzies, is very good at understanding where we are at any given time.
- Kevin Walsh, Managing Director of Biomediq from 1985 to-1988. He appointed me General Manager and let me manage the people as if the company was my own. I learned that getting results with people is sometimes more important than other priorities.

I am also inspired by every person within the Tanner Menzies team, and I learn something from them everyday. They are a fun-loving and hard working group of people.

No 1 Recruitment Success Secret

Look after your candidate! Treat them like gold and remember that they may well be your future client. In this business a candidate is just as valuable as a client and they should all be treated with honesty and integrity.

No 1 Manager's Success Secret

Look after your people! As far as I am concerned Tanner Menzies is not me, it is the people I work with. If you value their contribution you will work to inspire them to succeed beyond their dreams.

Attributes of Top Recruiters

The top recruiters will be identifiable by these characteristics:
- Persistence – Hang in there and be tenacious. Have a dogged determination to get the job done, accompanied by a sense of humour.
- The ability to bounce back – It is in your blood, and success is something which feels really good.
- Intelligence – You need to have the ability to solve problems quickly and to think laterally.
- Empathy – You are dealing with your fellow mankind and it is important to be able to understand where they are and what they are seeking to achieve.

Advice to Recruiters Wanting To Be The Best

If you want to be the best you have to believe in yourself first. Then you must make sure that the company you work for believes in you and supports you 100 per cent. If you believe you are the best and that your efforts are recognised, then you will always give your absolute best.

Peter Tanner

Advice to Owners & Managers Growing A Business

Value your people and recognise the contribution they can make to your business. Make sure they understand and reflect your desired culture in the marketplace.

Treat your clients with respect and be fair in your dealings. It is essential to consistently deliver the highest standards and really add value to their business.

Career Lessons Learned

I can honestly say that there is nothing I would have done differently. I am happy with what we have at Tanner Menzies. I have done the best I can.

Recruitment in 2005

The industry will be very different. I envisage a combination of large organisations and smaller boutique search companies with no middle ground at all. The industry will shake out with lots of mergers and acquisitions.

The industry will be globally based with heavy Internet reliance. We won't see advertisements in the newspaper, apart from corporate advertisements directing people to agency and client Web sites. I believe the next generation will rely solely on the Internet for jobs. Recruiters will need to search and network diligently, placing even more reliance on a quality database.

Companies will outsource more and more and the industry will grow dramatically because of this. Recruiters will need to offer a range of Human Resource services, including contracting, which will continue to grow as the workforce becomes more flexible.

The industry needs to become more regulated. We are responsible for the psychological well-being of people and I don't believe there is enough control over who is working in our industry. The industry will be judged on the reputation of our worst member who will pull everyone down. We must look harder at assisting our clients with selection because their company performance is affected by the people we recommend to do the job.

We need to support each other within the industry and deliver a unified message to our clients and potential clients. That message is that we have value to bring to the recruitment equation.

Janet Vallino

Recently inducted into the RCSA Queensland Hall of Fame, Janet Vallino has carved out an important role in recruiting and in Australian business.

Hailing from rural North Queensland Janet joined the industry as a trainee consultant in 1975 with Key Personnel which, after several mergers and acquisitions, has been known as Alfred Marks, Adia, Adia Centacom and now Adecco.

Throughout the years Janet has moved from consulting to senior positions such as Branch Manager, Regional Manager and Training Manager for the one organisation, surviving the challenges of constant change.

Janet Vallino

She has been recognised many times through awards and nominations. Janet was a finalist in the Telstra Business Woman of the Year 1997 and recipient of a Women of Substance Award in 1998. Within Adecco her unique contribution has been widely honoured, with the Outstanding Achiever in Australia Award in 1990, Outstanding Manager in 1994 and the KJJ Award in 1995, the company's most prestigious internal award, bestowed on employees whose achievements have been extraordinary.

A keen participant in the wider industry Janet has held senior positions including National Director for the NAPC, (now the RCSA), Queensland Chair of the IPC (the education arm of the NAPC), Queensland Councillor of AHRI and Secretary of the Australian Telecommunications Association.

Janet's contributions to the community through volunteer work are extensive and she has generously given her time to promote various awards schemes. As well as judging the Telstra/ATA awards from 1996-1999 she also judged the Multicap Mrs Australia Awards and Care Awards for ten years.

Her passionate approach is well-known and defines the way Janet applies herself to every part of her life, not just her career. It is seen in her love of gardening, her determination to write an autobiography and ultimately in her dedication to her grandchildren whom, she says, are the greatest love of her life.

With a view of the world that sees the glass as half full, not half empty, Janet has always worked hard to make things happen. Fuelled by a thirst for learning, a desire to be the best she can be and a passion for the recruitment industry, Janet has accepted the challenges thrown at her by constant change in her career.

Through recruitment Janet believes she is making a positive contribution to the community through helping candidates, clients and staff to transform their lives and their businesses.

Working with others has also been a source of motivation. As an active committee member of the RCSA and other organisations in the wider business community Janet has seen the importance of training, developing networks, encouraging and supporting others to ensure the best possible results.

Enjoyment Factors

This is a fast-paced dynamic industry that presents us with constant change and a variety of challenges. I love having the opportunity to learn and develop new skills, and the freedom to run my desk as if it were my own business.

First Interview

I enjoy being kept up to date with commerce and industry and having the chance to meet and network with people from all walks of life, as well as to share information with colleagues and learn from my competitors.

This is an exciting time to be involved in recruiting as well as managing the transition from an industrial age to an information age. There is a huge challenge in learning not just how to operate our business with new technology, but how to think differently as well.

In this role I see myself as a catalyst to help people identify new career opportunities, improve their careers and enhance their lifestyles. I love being in a situation which combines my natural ability and skill and also gives me the chance to keep learning to contribute to my own personal and professional growth.

Inspirational People

I am most inspired by people who overcome adversity and personal challenges, often through their enthusiasm and positive approach, integrity, work ethic and honesty.

I am also inspired by people who demonstrate an in-depth knowledge of the recruitment industry and contribute to the community and corporate world.

No 1 Recruitment Success Secret

The paramount secret to success in recruiting is empathy. Recruiters must have the ability to place themselves in the other person's position (candidates, clients, staff). It's about recognising that the total person is greater than the parts.

No 1 Manager's Success Secret

This comes down to integrity, total honesty and commitment in your dealings with other people, especially your staff. You are only as good as the people around you.

Attributes of Top Recruiters

This is a long list because to be at the top a recruiter has to be very special indeed.

They must have:
• Passion
• Integrity

- Empathy
- Flexibility
- Perception
- Sales flair
- Good relationship-building and listening skills
- A 'customer first' attitude
- Ability to adjust to change and go with the flow
- Initiative
- Creativity
- Time management/self-management.

They must be:
- Results-oriented
- Non-judgemental
- A lateral thinker
- Tenacious
- Persistent
- Energetic
- Driven from within to succeed
- Enthusiastic
- Ethical
- Committed and dedicated
- Able to multi-task
- Presented professionally – ready to look, think and act the role.

Advice to Recruiters Wanting To Be The Best

T E A M – Together Everyone Achieves More. It is the input that makes the output.

It's important to keep on learning. The way to achieve this is through seeking out opportunities with the RCSA, additional courses and seminars. Keep up to date with information and knowledge on industry, commerce, market trends and salaries and take ownership of your industry knowledge.

Get actively involved with relevant committees such as the ATA and AHRI. Networking is the way to learn from everyone – especially your competitors.

Build up psychological contracts with candidates and clients and stay one step ahead and surprise them by exceeding their expectations. At the very least, always do what you say you will do. Understand your candidate's wants and wishes and understand your client's business.

Lastly top recruiters need to have an entrepreneurial flair. Run the desk as if it were your own business. Set personal and professional goals and develop a life and business plan.

Advice to Owners & Managers Growing A Business

To business owners I would say this: It has to be done, but it must be fun.

Embrace change and innovation and don't be afraid to identify new niche markets. Focus on your core business. Don't be a machine gun, be a bow and arrow.

Have respect for the recruitment industry and your competitors. Recruit good people – train, support, encourage, recognise the individual strengths of your staff and build on these. Training and mentoring team spirit will boost staff morale and critical empowerment, leading to better staff retention and loyalty of service.

Set clear goals. Value consistency and fairness and provide recognition and rewards for these things.

Career Lessons Learned

I have learned to appreciate the importance of balancing a career with a personal and family life. You can have a successful career and still enjoy a good quality of life.

The other lesson I have learned is to never underestimate your own ability and value.

Recruitment in 2005

Due to the impact of globalisation we will see more big players, global recruitment contracts and fewer middle-sized consultancy firms.

Internet recruitment will make the industry more sophisticated and thanks to technology, more consultants will work from home.

To embrace the future of the industry the RCSA needs to adopt a slightly different focus that takes technology into account and allows them to think globally while still acting locally.

The RCSA will benefit from broadening its scope to include areas such as ER, IR, discrimination and outplacement. By looking at a far bigger picture on business the RCSA will come to terms with a total service for business, electing leadership in each state who can interact with global, international, national and all niche markets.

Paul Veith

Paul Veith is Managing Director of IPA Group, an international company operating in a number of areas of recruitment. Paul established IPA in May 1984 via a unique franchising concept which attracted top consultants and enjoyed astonishing growth.

He expanded the company with IPA Healthcare in 1992, which grew rapidly and sold to its UK partner in 1999, on target to place 2000 Australians and New Zealanders in the UK.

Paul Veith

In 1992 Paul's vision for countering cyclical unemployment saw him focused on the placement of disadvantaged job seekers through the Department of Education and Training. IPA recently won a tender to provide Government funded employment services from 54 sites throughout Australia which, when added to existing sites, comprises the largest full service recruitment network in Australia.

He joined the industry in 1970 with Drake International in Toronto, Canada and has held a number of senior positions there and in the UK. As well as his work with IPA he was involved in the rebirth of Catalyst Recruiting Services in 1990 and purchased Lawstaff in 1992.

Paul's motivation comes from a number of factors. As the youngest in his family he says he was always motivated to succeed. He had a strong sense of enterprise and held a number of part-time jobs while still quite young.

Paul is still impacted by the example of his grandfather who came to Sydney from America in 1918 and settled in a house called "Perseverando".

He derives great satisfaction from helping other people to achieve and gets really excited about moving an idea from concept to action through taking calculated risks.

Enjoyment Factors

I greatly enjoy working with the people in the recruitment industry. They are invariably dynamic, hard working and have a good sense of humour. I really like the limitless opportunities the recruitment industry provides.

I have learned that there are no limits apart from those we impose on ourselves. All recruiters have access to the same employers and applicants, therefore success is only limited by the individual – it is always the person that makes the difference.

Inspirational People

Among the many people I could name I have to include Diane Eleoff from Drake in Toronto who was the greatest ever trainer of permanent consultants. She taught me that consultants have the responsibility to provide maximum service to both candidates and employers – always giving a little bit extra.

Also Noel Wheeler, my area manager at Drake, Melbourne 1974-1977, taught me more about people management than anybody else. He was extremely good at recognising achievement and very prompt at identifying opportunities for improvement. I have endeavoured to emulate this management style.

No 1 Recruitment Success Secret

Without hesitation I would say honesty. There are too many consultants who are not honest. The best consultant will talk a client out of hiring a particular person if they are not the right candidate for the job.

No 1 Manager's Success Secret

Focus 90 per cent of your energy on revenue generation. Revenue is everything because it gives you the freedom to mold your organisation as you would like, even though you may appear to be 'cheap' while keeping expenses down.

Attributes of Top Recruiters

Clearly the best recruiters can probe clients and applicants, always asking why, to drill down to the true needs of the people being interviewed.

A good recruiter never files away good candidates who have not been placed. That's a waste of quality people. This business is very, very simple – just difficult to do. Good consultants think laterally and don't waste resources given to them by their employers.

Advice to Recruiters Wanting To Be The Best

Successful consultants need to emulate what the best recruiters do that works. Then they will add their own knowledge for even better performance.

Advice to Owners & Managers Growing A Business

My advice to managers relates to the way you treat your people. Firstly you have to remember that you cannot motivate people, you can only facilitate them.

Make your staff very aware of what the organisation expects in return for the salary paid. Encourage staff to come to you with solutions not problems. Effective managers will ask people to assess their own work or performance so that they can learn for themselves rather than relying on being told.

Use placement ratios and KPIs to help people boost their success rates. Encourage consultants to analyse their own ratios and develop ideas to increase their placement rates.

Success depends on the actions of your people so give credit, don't take credit. From the day you open your business you are the average of the people who report to you. Managers must encourage the performance of others giving them the recognition that previously you needed yourself.

Only two things will affect someone's performance – willingness and ability. If someone is willing but not able then training will help them to become a good staff member. However if they are able but not willing, refer them to an employment opportunity that does not require results.

Career Lessons Learned

Next time round I would not be sucked in by people's potential if they don't have inner drive. I have persevered with some people for too long; people who had the ability but not the willingness or the enthusiasm.

I would have expanded faster by bringing in additional management earlier. I would also have brought in a partner sooner so I could focus on what I enjoy doing rather than what the business needed.

The big lesson I've learned has to do with having the courage to delegate the tasks you don't do well, and not punishing yourself for the weaknesses you have.

Recruitment in 2005

Looking at different industry sectors:
- I think industrial recruitment will continue to boom as companies seek to outsource and contract out blue-collar work.
- Secretarial and office support will be predominantly temporary with the possible exception of call centres that will maintain a degree of permanent staff.
- Executive technical will continue to boom but with increased reliance on the Internet.
- Healthcare will follow the trends of the UK; we will see nurse banks managed by the employment industry.

There is strong potential for our industry to deliver solutions more than just people. We should stop selling bodies and provide companies with productivity-based packages and functionality.

We need to become more consultative in our approach and understand IR and OH&S issues. It is going to be about providing even better service to increasingly more sophisticated clients.

Peter Waite

Peter Waite is Chief Executive of the Waite Group, a recruitment company established by his father in 1959. The company's first advertisement for an assignment appeared in the newspaper on the day Peter was born so it is true to say he has been involved in the business since Day One.

After his father's death in 1968, Peter's mother Noel took over the business making her one of Australia's first women business-owners within the recruitment industry. Noel set the example of good business values which have characterised Peter's career.

Peter Waite

After some years working for Mobil Oil in Far North Queensland Peter entered the business in 1983 and cut his teeth on low level recruitment. He became Managing Director in 1987, aged 28. He started to build the business, extending the core service of Executive Recruitment with entry into the temporary and office support market in 1989 and later Noel Waite formalised outplacement and career development.

The Waite Group is a boutique HR services provider with 35 staff specialising in middle to senior management in financial services, telecommunications and government and utilities. With offices in Canberra and Melbourne, and associates in Asia, the company also works in HR outsourcing for small to medium enterprises and family businesses.

Highlights include beating 13 competitors to win a large national Telstra contract to recruit 5,000 people in 1995 and recently moving a team of seven client advisors from one global stock broking firm to another using executive search methodology.

Peter takes pride in the Waite Group's low staff turnover and longevity. He attributes his staff loyalty to the Group's family values and cultural fit. As a break from the business Peter spends time on his farm with his young family in Tallarook in northern Victoria where he breeds black angus cattle and fat lambs. He finds this relaxing and says, "Working with animals is more predictable than people."

A lot of Peter's motivation has come from the desire to maintain and add value to the good name Waite has held in the market for many years. That means carrying on the family tradition of helping people with their careers and being renowned for doing complete and successful assignments which will bring repeat business.

He says that he was brought up in a way that made him hungry for success with rewards for his efforts coming not just from money but also from the joy of seeing clients and candidates become partners and friends.

Enjoyment Factors

I love this business and all it involves: making successful placements, seeing careers flourish, meeting diverse people and gaining exposure to a broad range of industries.

And although it's not my prime motivation this is definitely the best industry for making money. I really enjoy pitching for and winning business and seeing good rewards for turning around assignments quickly.

Inspirational People

I have been inspired by people from all parts of my life. My mother has been a fantastic role model and mentor. We have worked together for 17 years and being on the same wavelength has really helped. We tend to have complimentary skills. She is more creative while I am more business-driven. She has passed on strong values, diligence and a real commitment to individuals.

Elsewhere I have benefited from knowing a number of offshore people in Asia and the US who have given me ideas about business and structural operations. An exposure to international students, while studying my MBA, prompted me to explore search partners in the Asian markets. The Executive Connection has been very inspirational because it can be lonely at the top and it's great to share and learn with other chief executives.

No 1 Recruitment Success Secret

A recruiter needs to have the ability to read people, to know what makes them tick and quickly sum up whether they are the right client or candidate. This is really about good judgment – it's not easy to learn and is usually best demonstrated by women as they have strong intuition.

No 1 Manager's Success Secret

Business owners should employ the best people in the industry with values that are compatible to the business. Do not put up with mediocrity in terms of performance.

Attributes of Top Recruiters

The primary attribute of a top recruiter is definitely empathy. This means having good listening skills, asking open-ended questions, looking for competencies not just skills and experience. Past behaviour is a good predictor of future behaviour.

Also consultants need to have tenacity especially when researching information on candidates and reference checking. Ensure that you match candidates to the right job in the right company.

Positive people with genuine and warm personalities do best. They should also be consultative, add value to clients and not just be there for the sale. I can't overemphasise the need to obtain the trust of clients and candidates.

Peter Waite

Advice to Recruiters Wanting To Be The Best

Join a firm that will give you growth, keeping in mind that this often does not happen in big firms. Look for a mentor and immerse yourself in training and constant learning.

Make sure you are diligent in the recruitment process. Consider getting corporate experience in HR first as it is always easy to get into recruitment consulting. When it is time do your homework about who to join and get some good mentors.

Advice to Owners & Managers Growing A Business

Employ the best people you can find and attract or grow your own. Often a combination of people can work well.

Be uncompromising with your standards and company values. Simply don't put up with mediocrity. It sounds harsh but it's better to 'cut the cancer'.

If you can, expedite the process of devolving yourself from operational and hands-on recruiting and step back so that you are free to work on the business, not in the business. Take calculated entrepreneurial risks so that you can grow the business more quickly.

Career Lessons Learned

Ideally I would have had more corporate experience when I started out instead of jumping into the industry at the age of 23.

However I have learned some valuable lessons along the way. A business should have a broad client base and not rely on a few major clients. Don't get locked into high volume, low margin contracts and stay away from prospective clients who want you to discount. They will often give you a hard time throughout the assignment and you will find you are better off without them!

Choose your clients – don't let them choose you.

Recruitment in 2005

There will be many more mergers and acquisitions in the future and, later on, more floats. There will be two forms of players – global and niche. Anyone in the middle will be in real trouble. Niche players will be able to charge premium prices and make more money per consultant than the international players. Despite this shake-out of firms in the middle ground I think the industry will continue to grow strongly.

Online recruitment will continue to grow and take market share over traditional advertising. Firms will continue to get more unsolicited applicants from job boards but should be aware this does not necessarily mean better quality.

The job of recruitment is becoming more difficult because clients are demanding faster service due to the perception that online technology and job boards are providing more candidates, more information, more quickly. The reality is that mobiles and email are making our lives faster, not necessarily better!

Looking at demographics and our ageing population there will be a growing, continued shortage of candidates. Firms who can build candidate loyalty and value could be in a commanding position. There will also be a lot more HR outsourcing of recruitment and other HR services as firms continue to downsize their mid-level HR staff.

George Zammit

George Zammit is Managing Director of Catalyst Recruitment Systems, one of Australia's largest industrial recruiting companies with operations in every mainland state and a current turnover of $60 million. Catalyst commenced operations in 1991 and the company has enjoyed continual growth ever since, culminating in its listing on the Australian Stock Exchange in June 1999.

George started in the recruitment industry with Drake Consulting in 1974 in Melbourne. The following year he was moved to Perth to take up the position of State Manager of the Group's Western Australian operations.

George Zammit

By 1987 George's responsibilities were Australia-wide and involved him in all facets of decision-making for the Group. In 1988 he was made a Director and was transferred to London as Chief Executive of the Group's UK and European operations.

He enjoyed the challenge of learning to understand international cultures and labour regulations and later went on to become responsible for the industrial and medical divisions worldwide.

George has worked closely with at least 12 people who have since become very senior in the industry, no doubt influenced by his determination, encouragement and mentorship.

As far as George is concerned recruitment is unique in that it is a personal performance industry – it is your level of success that allows you to move forward. This has been an important source of motivation for him and he has seen people move quickly through the ranks based on their performance.

He is also driven by the potential growth of the industry, especially considering the penetration of recruitment by companies is only 20 per cent in Australia compared with 40-50 per cent in the US.

Apart from these factors George never lost sight of the fact that he had three children to feed and a mortgage to service – strong motivators indeed.

Enjoyment Factors

I really enjoy the people – this is an industry that values people and makes the most of opportunity to train and develop them very quickly, allowing them to move ahead of their peers.

I enjoy the rapid rate of change and the competitive nature of the industry because you are never safe from people trying to take business from you.

I feel I am good at running a recruitment business, and this helps me enjoy it. In concept, the recruitment process sounds easy, but it is hard to do.

Inspirational People

Many people with whom I have worked in the industry have inspired me over the years. Some of these are competitors – adversaries but not enemies.

There are many people who have inspired me to dare to be good. Wanting to be as good as these people helped to stir my competitive nature.

No 1 Recruitment Success Secret

Get the order and find a way to fill it. Our approach is a little different to other companies – we target outsourced business and would like to take over the whole job e.g. a production line or a warehouse. We are really in the business of handling workloads and finding people to do that work. This has allowed us to grow at a compounded rate of 34 per cent each year.

No 1 Manager's Success Secret

My success in business management has been through identifying the right people to work with – Catalyst has grown predominantly with people who had never been in the industry. We train and develop and motivate the people to high levels. This encourages our consultants to go beyond normal hours and allows us to respond to our clients 24 hours a day. Our internal systems and people are critical to our success.

Attributes of Top Recruiters

You need the ability to generate work rather than process work given to you. This is not necessarily selling but a philosophy that says, "Give me the tools I need and I will run my desk like a business."

People who have strong follow-up skills and systems are successful. High energy levels are also very important. Very few successful recruiters work fewer than 10-12 hours a day, minimum 5 days a week. Successful recruiters also have the ability to make a lasting and positive impact on people. People who are seen truly as consultants and not sales people will do the best.

Consultants need courage in the face of constant change and rejection. Remember you are working with an imperfect product – people!

You need to be able to communicate the real picture to people about the practical aspects and reality of the job, the labour market and environmental issues. A good recruiter will have the skill and intuition to accurately match the environmental and cultural needs of the applicant and client.

You have to want to be Number One; to have the instinct to be the best in a team. Unfortunately, second is only ever the best of the losers.

Advice to Recruiters Wanting To Be The Best

Firstly you must realise that you can only generate business from 9-5, when the client is available. Any other support or administration work must be done outside those hours, when clients are not available.

You need a system to maximise the effectiveness of your inputs. This business is a mathematical formula. Perhaps you can influence 100 people and end up doing business with one person. Then if you can impact 1000 people your business will increase 10 times.

Identify motivators for people using your service. Learn to speak the same language as your clients and match their needs beyond skill requirements. It's a mistake to spend too much time focusing on skills – look at how the person fits in with the client's culture and personality.

Finally, I think a good recruiter must be self motivated and have the ability to manage the boss so you keep feeling special and don't end up becoming average.

Advice to Owners & Managers Growing A Business

Lead by example – don't tell them, show them! If you have the right people, they don't need a boss. Give your people a track to run on – a broad game plan which they can contribute to.

Provide staff training so they are developing their needs as well as the business. Training should encompass personal development such as time and stress management.

As a manager you need to be visible, working the hours you expect your people to do also. You should promote a demonstrated policy that you don't discriminate in any way among staff and candidates.

Make sure you are focused on the business of the future. While your consulting team is focused on today's events, the management team and sales people must have their eye on tomorrow's events, management particularly, so that the company grows.

I see my primary role at Catalyst is to make the telephone ring. Managers should create an inventory of what everyone does best and make sure this is how they spend their time.

Personally I think it's important to have significant overlap between your business and personal life. My desk is still in the kitchen so I can be around my family. At Catalyst we fill 60 job orders between 7pm-7am each week.

Career Lessons Learned

I was with Drake for nearly 17 years and looking back I should have left them a lot earlier. Even though I learned an enormous amount there I learned three times that in the first two years at Catalyst.

For example, I learned that managing cashflow is critical when running your own company. I also learned many things leading up to the Catalyst float – probably the steepest learning curve of my career so far.

I would have not franchised the other states outside Sydney and Melbourne, as it is not possible to control and manage culture and standards within the confines of a franchise. The rate of growth has been enormous since ending the franchise arrangement.

I probably would have developed a big company structure earlier and might have set up Catalyst's head office in Sydney not Melbourne because the Sydney market is bigger and, although I visit often, it is not the same as living there.

Recruitment in 2005

There is definite growth in the future with an increased penetration to business growing by 2-3 per cent each year. We will also have a more deregulated environment because the concept of contract works is becoming more readily acceptable.

The surviving organisations will be those with good control over OH&S, particularly in the labour hire sector, which continues to grow faster than the executive sector. The five largest recruiters in the world are predominantly industrial recruiters.

The industry will be fragmented into niche markets and small players will specialise more e.g. in the US there is a company which only recruits sales people for outdoor furniture companies.

We will see clients demanding more than just labour – they want training, supervision and induction systems and responsibility for outcomes. The largest users of contract labour will buy or set up their own agencies and service themselves, similar to Andersen Contracting.

The big thing is that the industry needs to stop competing with itself and undercutting other recruiters. We have to start competing with the 80 per cent of the market that doesn't use us. I'd like to see us, as an industry, deciding how can we work together to increase our market size.

Online recruitment advertising tools that give recruiters a richer experience.

adenergy.com.au

Australia's most energetic recruitment advertising agency now provides a 24 hour, 7 days a week online service.

Just Press for Action!

You can even check your recruitment company share prices! (http://www.adenergy.com.au/economicind.htm)

Join the leaders in the Recruitment Industry

Make a commitment to your future and to the recruitment and consulting services industry.

• Show your professionalism • Grow with strength • Stay informed • Participate

RCSA members abide by a Code of Professional Conduct, are committed to ongoing education and Professional Development and the development of Industry Standards.

The RCSA supports its members through a wide range of services to keep members abreast of information on industry issues, trends, best practice techniques, resources and technological innovation, along with legislative changes impacting on employment.

Division Councils provide excellent forums for members to directly influence the shaping of the industry through participation in a range of special interest groups and committees.

A variety of local seminars, updates, short courses, networking and social functions such as the Annual Conference are provided to ensure members stay informed.

The RCSA suite of publications ensures access to sound and accurate information to underpin the multiple roles the industry fulfils. The Recruitment Journal provides an invaluable insight into the industry, and publications such as the RCSA Industry Handbook and OH&S booklet are vital reference tools for recruitment practitioners.

The website www.rcsa.com.au delivers a myriad of industry specific information, including tailored products and services.

The RCSA has an ongoing commitment to members through the development of a range of business partnerships to assist in improving the range and quality of member services.

For further information contact RCSA on (03) 9614 5455 or visit the website at www.rcsa.com.au.

Recruitment & Consulting Services Association

Representing and servicing the interests of members for the increased profile and professionalism of the industry.

Order form

Recruitment Industry Performance Reports

The most important reports you will ever need.

Over 60 pages with 65 performance indicators and recruitment industry market trends. Stay ahead of your competition by moving towards industry best practice and lifting your firm to the highest standards.

- Ensure your firm is operating at the leading edge of the industry
- Compare your firm with up-to-date operating benchmarks
- Instantly highlight areas for potential improvement
- Check on leading financial ratios
- Plan your company growth based on industry operating standards
- Know the attributes of the top performing consultants and where to find them

---

The Recruitment Industry Performance Report contains survey results from profitable recruitment firms covering

- Recruitment market trends
- Commission structures

- Placement conversion rates
- Marketing activities
- Media response levels
- Key performance indicators
- Pricing and margins
- Financial benchmarks
  And many more...

Fax or mail this page to Navigator Consulting, Suite 17, 1 Cranbrook Ave, Cremorne NSW 2090, Australia. Fax 02 9904 4642. Tel 02 9904 1474

Sydney Recruitment Industry Performance Report

☐ **$495** RCSA Member (Incl 10% GST) ☐ **$660** Non RCSA Member (Incl 10% GST)

Melbourne Recruitment Industry Performance Report

☐ **$495** RCSA Member (Incl 10% GST) ☐ **$660** Non RCSA Member (Incl 10% GST)

Both Reports ☐ **$900** (Prices include GST and FREE Postage)

Amount charged - $.....................

Method of payment

BC ☐   MC ☐   VISA ☐   CHEQUE ☐

Card Number ☐☐☐☐ ☐☐☐☐ ☐☐☐☐ ☐☐☐☐

Expiry Date ☐☐ ☐☐

Name on card .... Signature ....

Your report(s) will be mailed to you immediately upon payment.

Your Name .... Ms/Mr/Mrs etc ....

Company .... Position ....

Address .... Postcode ....

Suburb .... Phone ....

E-mail .... Fax ....

Nomination form – Our next book
Second Interview by Tony Hall

Success secrets from recruitment industry rising stars and quiet achievers.

Please nominate up to 5 active recruitment professionals who you think are poised to lead the industry and whose success will provide inspiration to others.

Nomination 1 .... Company ....

Nomination 2 .... Company ....

Nomination 3 .... Company ....

Nomination 4 .... Company ....

Nomination 5 .... Company ....

Fax or mail this page to Navigator Consulting, Suite 17, 1 Cranbrook Ave, Cremorne NSW 2090, Australia. Fax 02 9904 4642. Tel 02 9904 1474

Please insert your details.

Name ....

Position .... Title ....

Address ....

....

Phone .... Fax ....

Email ....